Ask the Doctor
Depression

Ask the Doctor
Depression

Vincent Friedewald, M.D.
with Julie Stockler
Foreword by Mike Wallace

Vincent E. Friedewald III
Series Editor

**Andrews McMeel
Publishing**
Kansas City

www.andrewsmcmeel.com

98 99 00 01 02 BAH 10 9 8 7 6 5 4 3 2 1

Library of Congress Cataloging-in-Publication Data

Friedewald, Vincent E., 1941–
    Ask the doctor : depression / Vincent Friedewald
    and Julie Stockler; foreword by Mike Wallace
        p.   cm.
    Includes index
    ISBN 0-8362-2711-5 (pbk.)
    1. Depression, Mental—Popular works. I. Stockler, Julie
II. Title.
RC537.F725   1998
616.85'27—dc21   97–39089
                              CIP

Contents

Foreword

Nourish Your Brain
by Mike Wallace

Interviewing people is my love, my life's work, and through the years with the *60 Minutes* cameras rolling I've had my share of satisfying encounters. But there have been a few that didn't measure up.

Perhaps the worst episode was back in 1985, with no cameras, no producers, no writers present. Just me and a psychiatrist who'd been treating me for depression. It was one of the few crucial times in my life when I failed to ask the right questions, and I didn't listen closely enough to the answers.

With literally thousands of individuals I've interviewed over forty years, I was prepared. I did research about them ahead of time to gain insight into their past, their passions, their inspirations.

But in March of 1985, seated across from my psychiatrist, I didn't listen well enough, and I failed to ask him the right questions. Recovering from my first episode of depression, feeling so relieved and so satisfied that I was on the way back from the pit, I told the doctor I wanted to stop taking my medication, that I was tired of it, that it upset my stomach, whatever. As far as I was concerned, I was cured. I'd beaten the depression—albeit in one hell of a battle, but I was cured. And so I didn't listen to my doctor's warnings. "Mr. Wallace, it's really best you stick with it for a few more months." I didn't hear him, I didn't feel the need to ask follow-up questions; after all, I thought, who takes a drug when he doesn't feel sick?

I stopped the medication for my depression against his advice and within a matter of weeks it all came back full force. Or rather, *stormed* back. Playing tennis one day—one glorious day—I fell and broke my wrist, and without warning, the depression—somehow— was back. Devastating! I was totally unprepared. This time just as bad as the first time.

That's when I began to ask myself—and the doctor—a lot more questions about depression. What *is* this disease, exactly; why did I have it? Would it keep coming back for the rest of my life? Could this hell be prevented?

I learned all I could about depression, read about it, talked about it with my doctor, with my wife, Mary, and with others who'd been there, my friends William Styron and Art Buchwald, who had also agonized through the darkness. And most important, I learned a lot about my medication. The doctor explained to me just what it had been doing for my brain; that the medicine was actually feeding chemicals into my brain, chemicals my brain apparently had stopped manufacturing for itself. And without those chemicals, I became depressed. But with them . . . a huge difference.

Fact is, I no longer think of my antidepressant as medication, instead I like to think of it as *nourishment*. The antidepressant *nourishes* the brain.

From what I've come to realize, a *lot* of people learn that the hard way. They misunderstand depression and the role of medication, and as a result, they're reluctant to undertake it, or they stop taking it before it's had a chance fully to nourish their brain. I understand why they stop. Face it: Treatment can be frustrating, with awkward side effects, inconvenient dosages, times when nothing seems to help, nothing seems to be changing.

But hang in there, to anyone being treated for depression: You can recover, you *will* recover, but you've got to stay with your medication until your doctor says it's time. *Nourish your brain*. Give it what it needs.

And learn more about depression. Share *Ask the Doctor: Depression* with your family, so they'll know better what to expect and why.

Learning, listening, asking the right questions—*knowing what to expect and why*—that's what gets us through depression. That's what allows us to live our lives again.

How to Use
Ask the Doctor
Depression

First, read the book cover to cover. Don't worry about remembering every detail the first time through. Be sure to answer the "It's Your Turn" questions at the end of each section. These questions are designed to help the book suit *your* needs, and will help you get more involved with understanding depression.

Then keep *Ask the Doctor: Depression* readily available, as a reference for use in the future. Make special note of the icons in the margins: These not only mark issues that we feel are especially important to the discussion, but also will help you move quickly to certain parts of the book later on.

And for more convenience, *Ask the Doctor: Depression* is written so that it can be picked up and read from any point. This way you can share certain parts with family members or friends without them having to read the entire book. Of course, we encourage everyone to learn as much as possible about depression, for understanding this disease is the key to defeating it. For this same reason, we also encourage you to make use of the appendix, which lists and describes numerous support groups dedicated to helping people overcome depression.

Finally, remember that *Ask the Doctor: Depression*, though filled with useful and medically safe information, is never a substitute for your doctor. Only your doctor, who knows you better than we do anyway, should be the final judge about how you should take care of your health.

Icons

Throughout *Ask the Doctor: Depression*, you will see a number of icons, symbols in the margin of the page used to emphasize important information. We have arranged the icons in such a way that it is very easy to use them as reference guides. For example, if you wish to read only about the genetic aspects of depression, you can page though the book and look for all the paragraphs with the Family History/Genetic Risk icon. The same goes for all of the icons pictured below.

 Brain Chemistry

 Family History/Genetic Risk

 Notable Terminology

 Medication/Drugs

 Stress-Related Topics

 Caution! Important Information

 Time

 Ask Your Doctor/ Talk to Your Doctor

 Recurrence

 Suicide

 Age-specific

Psychotherapy

 Female

It's Your Turn

Ask the Doctor
Depression

1

What Is Depression?

It's a Disease

Do you believe that your last bout with the flu was triggered by a character flaw? That your hay fever comes from a lack of willpower? That you need glasses because you have too many negative thoughts?

Of course not.

You know that influenza, allergy, and poor eyesight have *nothing* to do with how "strong" you are and *everything* to do with viruses, pollen, and weak eye muscles. In spite of the mind-body connection we hear so much about, it should be easy to spot a real disease when we see one.

But it isn't so easy. Especially with a disease like depression.

People with depression have a disease that's every bit as "real" as an infection or an allergy. The chief cause of depression is a chemical imbalance in the brain. Just like a viral infection in the throat makes it difficult for you to swallow, the changes in the chemical activity of the brain can make you depressed, as well as make it difficult to think, behave, or feel the way we should.

But because these symptoms mainly involve our mood, depression does not seem like a *real* disease at all. And since it doesn't make you bleed, limp, or sweat, it's perfectly natural that you would try to cure yourself of depression by sheer force of the will.

Still not convinced? Let's look at some other diseases that you'd have to admit are genuine threats to our lives. Cancers of the lung, breast, colon, and prostrate (just to name a few) usually have no symptoms until they have advanced pretty far. Heart attacks may destroy large amounts of heart muscle without causing the slightest twinge of pain. And anemia has to become pretty serious before there is any fatigue.

What this means is that disease—even serious disease—can be present even if we can't *see* or *feel* any signs of it. However, when symptoms eventually do occur, those that affect our emotions are every bit as "real" as those that affect our bodies. Take Parkinson's disease, for example. The earliest symptoms of this disease are not physical problems, but rather changes in mood and behavior.

We can't say it enough. Even though they center around the mood, the symptoms of depression are nevertheless symptoms of a disease.

Hopefully, you are convinced. Now let's take a look at some important facts about depression.

The disease.

It's More than the Blues

To most people, depression means feeling sad.

But to physicians and other mental health professionals, depression is much more than that. Even though they most often refer to it simply as *depression* (which is how we will refer to it throughout this book), depression is a real disease to which doctors have given official-sounding names like *major depressive disorder* or *unipolar depression*. And just like any other disease, depression causes a specific set of symptoms. The problem that most people call depression—a sad mood—is actually just one symptom of this important disease. In fact, because there are many symptoms associated with depression, doctors have laid down a useful set of guidelines to help them determine exactly when they're looking at a patient who suffers from more than "the blues."

Doctors have decided that the diagnosis of depression requires at least five of the following symptoms to be present during the same period of time. Chapter 2 will explore these symptoms in detail.

- a sad mood

- an inability to feel pleasure from your favorite activities

- weight changes

- abnormal sleeping patterns

- restlessness or inactivity

- fatigue or loss of energy

- feelings of worthlessness or guilt

- an inability to think clearly

- thoughts about dying

When you think about it, there probably isn't anyone who hasn't felt at least some of these symptoms at some time. It's just the way our minds and our bodies react to life's negative stuff, like the loss of someone or something important to you. But there are big differences between feeling down, feeling disappointed, or even feeling grief-stricken, and having depression.

And just what are the differences? Most important, when you have depression, the symptoms don't go away after what we'd consider a reasonable period of time.

Here's an example. Let's say you've recently suffered the death of a very important person in your life. You may cry a lot, be unable to sleep or eat, and find yourself completely uninterested in any of the things that used to make your life tick. That reaction is *grief,* and it is a normal and necessary component of the healing process. As you recover, you'll eventually return to life. Not right away. Not without the occasional "bad day." But, on balance, you will ultimately have a scar in place of a gaping wound.

But a person with depression never really seems to heal. Several months after the loss—the period psychologists tend to believe signals the end of the normal period of intense grieving—he or she is still suffering profoundly.

A second difference is that depression often returns, sometimes in patterns of monthly depression followed by periods—maybe even years—of well-being.

Finally, depression often has no "trigger." Unlike grief, which follows a bad event, depression can just "happen" when everything is going just fine.

Who Gets Depression?

About one in twenty Americans each year. That's more than thirteen million people.

More than half of these people experience their first episode of the disease sometime between the ages of twenty and fifty. But a lot of children and teenagers—more than we realize—have depression. And it's quite common in the elderly, too. Bottom line: You can develop depression at any age.

If you're a female, you deserve special mention. Regardless of your country or culture, you're at least twice as likely as a man to get depression.

Men face about a 7 to 12 percent chance they'll suffer an episode of depression; for women, this lifetime risk may be as high as 25 percent. How come? For a long time, the medical community just assumed those numbers reflected the fact that women are more likely than men to seek professional help for health problems. (It's true.) But studies that specifically take this factor into account still come up with the same result: Women are twice as likely as men to have depression.

Why? We don't know for sure, but there are probably a lot of reasons at work. For example, women have a very different hormonal structure, and we know that hormones play a big role in depression. It's also possible that societies demand that women deal with stress differently than men, in ways that are more likely to bring on depression. The physical impact of childbirth is another possibility.

Generation "D"?

If the current trend continues, we can expect to see more and more young people with depression. Since World War II, the first episode of depression has been occurring at younger and younger ages. The greatest increase in the number of people with depression has been in the under-twenty age group.

Risk Factors

When doctors talk about risk factors for a medical problem—like heart disease—we know they're just minutes away from one of those chats about losing weight and getting back on the exercise bike.

But when it comes to risk factors for depression, the chats aren't about things we're doing wrong (or not doing right), but instead they're simply about who we are. People who are at greatest risk for developing depression are those who have a family history of the disease, and people who have had prior episodes of depression themselves.

Other people at greatest risk for depression are those who:

• are female

• are under the age of forty

• have been diagnosed with other illnesses

• have previously attempted suicide

- have recently given birth (women in the postpartum period)

- have experienced stressful life events

- lack social support

- abuse alcohol or drugs

But it's important to realize that these are only aspects of ourselves and our lives that *increase* our chances for depression; they don't *guarantee* it. In other words, a person could have all of these and still not develop depression.

And the opposite is true as well. A person can suffer from depression and have none of these factors, just like a person of normal weight who gets plenty of exercise can still have a heart attack.

More Female Troubles

We've already told you that women are more likely to have depression than men. Unfortunately, there's more. At least one study suggests that depressed women are more likely to have *longer* episodes of depression than men if they

- are older

- have had less than a high school education

- have had problems with their marriage

For men, however, age, education, and marital history seem unrelated to their ability to recover quickly.

What Causes Depression?

Reading the depression statistics and risk factors might scare anyone into thinking that he or she will become depressed. After all, many people are women, a lot of people are under the age of forty, and most everyone has suffered from a stressful life event.

But there is more to depression than simply adding up risk factors. Depression appears to come about as a result of the interaction among at least three conditions: abnormalities in the chemistry of the brain; a genetic predisposition to having these abnormalities; and, finally, certain psychological and social factors that somehow put the whole disease process in gear.

To understand all this, let's take a closer look at the brain itself.

Your Brain

One of your brain's most important tasks is to observe and react to events inside and outside your body.

Around the clock, it receives signals from every single part of your body—from your eyes, ears, nose, and skin, from your muscles and your organs, from the largest to the smallest blood vessels.

And that's only part of its job.

The brain also sends back signals to all of these parts of your body, telling them how to respond. This interaction is how the brain regulates normal body functions ("incoming dinner . . . stomach stand by"), protects you from the hazards of your environment ("oncoming train . . . legs, run forward fast"), and heals you when the environment gets the upper hand ("boiling water on skin . . . rescue cells, go to the scene").

Finally, an area we know less about is how the various parts of the brain communicate with each other. This fascinating world of neuroscience is the newest frontier of scientific research, in which our newly acquired knowledge of depression is only the beginning.

How Does the Brain Work?

The brain carries on most of its work via an incredibly intricate highway of nerve cells, or *neurons*. The chemical messengers that travel up and down this information highway are

---

What's a Neuro?

The term *neuro* means anything that involves the *nervous system,* i.e., the brain, the spine, or the nerves. It refers to the basic unit of the nervous system: the *neuron,* one of the tens of billions of long, spidery cells that are to the brain what copper wire is to the telephone company. So *neurologists* diagnose and treat diseases of the nervous system and *neurosurgeons* operate on it. *Neuralgia* refers to pain stemming from the nerves themselves, and *neuritis* to nerve inflammation. And before Freud got hold of it, even *neurosis* meant, quite simply, a disease of the nerves.

called *neurotransmitters*. These chemical substances come in different shapes and sizes, and each carries a different type of message. Some neurotransmitters direct your body to speed things up. Others convince it to slow down. You've probably heard of one neurotransmitter: *adrenaline*. That's the chemical messenger that floods into the bloodstream when the brain senses danger. Adrenaline orders your heart to beat faster and allows your feet to move more swiftly.

But as fast, efficient, and vital to our very survival as neurotransmitters are, they aren't perfect. When things go wrong with the neurotransmitters, the brain fails to function properly.

For example, we now know that people with Parkinson's disease—a condition that makes it difficult to start or stop muscle contraction—have abnormally low numbers of neurons responsible for secreting *dopamine,* a neurotransmitter essential to normal movement.

Just as abnormal levels of neurotransmitters like dopamine can provoke physical symptoms, abnormalities in other neurotransmitters can cause emotional symptoms. This link between biology and behavior has completely transformed medicine. Like every other bodily function, our moods are at the mercy of our molecules.

Taking Pictures of Depression
Radiologists can actually see mental illness.

The PET scan (that stands for *positron emission tomography*) is a sophisticated imaging technique that shows in vivid color just how active and energetic different areas of the brain are. This has made PET a valuable diagnostic tool for epilepsy, Parkinson's disease, and other neurological disorders since about the mid-1980s.

PET scans of depressed patients are providing evidence that there's a biological basis to this disease, too. Patients who are depressed show abnormally low activity in the centers of the brain that control mood. The worse the disease, the lower the activity. And scans taken once the depression lifts, during treatment with antidepressant medications, are often normal.

Serotonin

When you're depressed, the molecule involved is the neurotransmitter *serotonin.*

Serotonin (for you Ph.D. chemists, its chemical alias is 5-hydroxytryptamine, or 5-HT) is a neurotransmitter that turns up not only in the brain, but virtually everywhere else in the body as well. It is truly a molecular jack-of-all-trades, causing blood vessels to constrict, blocking sensations of pain, regulating sleep, and shaping appetite, to name just a few of its activities.

Some of serotonin's most profound effects in the brain take place in the *limbic system,* a mysterious area of the brain in part responsible for helping us cope with stresses from the outside world. Abnormally low levels of serotonin in the brain have been found to be related to all kinds of unhealthy behavior. These include: overeating, aggression, alcoholism, and compulsive actions. No wonder one scientist who studied serotonin called it "the molecule that makes us civilized."

Serotonin also keeps us from becoming depressed.

In over thirty years of research, the same finding has emerged over and over again: depressed persons have abnormally low levels of serotonin in their brains. And that's not all. When depressed persons are given drugs that raise brain serotonin levels, they usually get better, and sometimes recover completely.

Now that we have uncovered a link between serotonin and depression, why can't we just straighten out this serotonin problem and wipe out depression altogether? Maybe we will: It appears that a big step was made when chemists and pharmacologists developed an entirely new generation of antidepressant medications

The Chemistry of Bedtime Milk

Your mother may not have been a neurochemist, but she was chemically correct in giving you milk and cookies before bedtime. Of course, there's no proven therapeutic benefits to Oreos, except that they do successfully entice kids into drinking their milk. But milk contains lots of *tryptophan,* which is one of the building blocks of serotonin . . . which helps make you sleepy.

Be grateful she didn't make you eat bedtime tuna fish—it also contains tryptophan and, theoretically, would work as well.

(the SSRIs—more about them later) designed to elevate brain serotonin levels. Although these drugs work remarkably well, not everyone can be cured . . . yet.

That's because the neurotransmitter network is itself an intricate communication system containing hundreds of different neurotransmitters. And each neurotransmitter can pass along more than one kind of message. At times, a neurotransmitter hands off the message to yet other molecules known as *second messengers* and eventually even *third messengers*.

How Did They Figure This Stuff Out?

While the Nobel Prize committee may not like to admit it, many important discoveries in medicine are accidental.

In the 1950s, doctors were commonly prescribing a medication known as *reserpine* for their patients with high blood pressure. While reserpine did a respectable job of lowering blood pressure, many of the folks taking this drug were not happy about it. In fact, they weren't happy about anything. Reports of severe depression in persons taking reserpine became widespread.

Meanwhile, doctors treating patients for tuberculosis also noticed something strange. A surprising number of patients who were taking a drug called *isoniazid* felt great. They ate well, slept well, and were in all-around good moods. And their high spirits had nothing to do with improvement in their tuberculosis, since some of these happier patients were physically no better off than before starting isoniazid.

Intrigued by this wonderful but unexpected side effect, investigators considered what would happen if they gave isoniazid to depressed patients. Sure enough, within weeks, their depression improved.

One drug that lowers mood . . . another drug that elevates it. Chemists put two and two together in the lab and soon discovered they were looking at two drugs with opposite effects on a single site. Reserpine depletes the brain's supply of serotonin and another neurotransmitter called *norepinephrine*. In contrast, they found that isoniazid increases the amounts of these same chemicals.

What followed has been explosion in research aimed at developing drugs that alter neurotransmitter activity, as well as helping peel back the mysteries of the brain itself.

So even though serotonin plays a key role in depression, we also know that many of these other substances in the brain are important, too. And until we learn more about them, we still won't fully understand depression or be able to cure everyone.

A Look Inside Your Genes

Genetic research is another exciting arena of medical progress, pinpointing the specific genes that cause diseases such as cystic fibrosis and Huntington's disease. While researchers have yet to put their fingers on a specific gene for depression (and they are looking), we know for sure that genes play more than an accidental role in your chances of getting the disease.

What's the evidence? If someone in your family has depression, you're much more likely to get the disease yourself. And the closer you are on the family tree to the depressed person, the greater the chance that you'll get the disease too. First-degree relatives (parents, siblings, or offspring) of depressed persons are about three times more likely to experience depression at some time in their lives than are people in nondepressed families.

But wait. Wouldn't living with a depressed parent be reason enough to become depressed as a child or later in life? Nature clearly plays an important role, but doesn't nurture also contribute to an individual's depression?

Perhaps, the geneticists answer. But they also point to studies of adopted children. Even when they have been raised from birth in

**Bipolar Disease and
the Family Tree**
Bipolar depression (commonly known as *manic depression*) makes a definite mark on the family tree. We know this from studies of twins. Identical twins are those that carry the same genetic "blueprint." If one identical twin suffers from the disease, chances are about 50 percent that the other twin will also have the disease. However, in fraternal twins (who are genetically different), the risk is only 10 percent—the same as it is for any set of siblings.

adoptive families where no one is depressed, children whose bio-logical parents have the disease are much more likely to exhibit depression at some point in their lives. So there is good reason to press the search for a gene (or genes) responsible for causing de-pression or at least a tendency to get it.

Psychological and Social Factors

Although exact genes for depression have not been clearly iden-tified, it's unlikely that merely having the gene guarantees you'll have depression. That's because what you inherit is mainly the *tendency* for depression to occur under the right circumstances. And that's where the nurture part comes back into the picture.

In individuals who have an inherited vulnerability for depres-sion, the first episode usually begins with some sort of stressful event. Psychiatrists call such events *psychosocial stressors*. The most common stressors include separation or abuse in childhood or ado-lescence, divorce, and the death of a spouse. Of course, these losses are devastating enough to trigger overwhelming sadness in anyone. But for people who have a genetic risk, these types of events may trigger prolonged and intense episodes of depression that are well beyond the boundaries of what psychiatrists define as normal sor-row or grief. Even stress that most people would consider very minor (like the broken wrist that Mike Wallace mentions in the fore-word to this book) may trigger depression in the susceptible person.

And that only makes the person who can't find any "normal" reason for feeling depressed feel even *more* depressed.

One theory is that the first or second episode of depression in response to a bad life event triggers the chemicals in the brain to slide into a permanent imbalance. Whatever exactly goes on in the brain, it is absolutely clear that the first episode of depression can put the disease firmly into place. As a result, it may come back with alarming predictability, and often in the absence of any stressful event.

Just look at the facts:

- At least half of all people who suffer a single episode of depres-sion will experience a second episode.

- Almost three out of four people (70%) who have had two episodes of depression will have a third episode.

• Almost everyone (90%) who has had three episodes of depression will suffer a fourth episode.

Other Causes of Depression

Medical Diseases

When depression occurs alone, it is called a *primary* form of the disease. But depression can also result from an unrelated medical disorder, an unfortunate side effect of another disease. When this happens, the depression is called *secondary,* and it usually comes about in one of two ways.

First, depression can be brought on by another disease *directly* —or, as doctors say, *biologically.* This means that certain illnesses themselves can alter the brain chemistry, resulting in depressive symptoms. Hypothyroidism, for example, is a disorder in which the thyroid doesn't secrete enough of its own hormone. A brain that doesn't get its daily dose of thyroid hormone starts to make some internal adjustments, and these changes, in turn, cause depressive symptoms.

Depression can also be caused by another disease *indirectly.* In this case, the negative thoughts and anxieties a person may have about being ill can trigger an episode of secondary depression. So the depression results from *psychological* instead of direct biological reasons. An example of this is cancer: As many as one in four cancer patients experiences an episode of depression. The isolation of a hospital room, poorly controlled pain, and financial worries are some of the factors that may lead cancer patients to depression.

The distinction between primary and secondary depression is important in terms of treatment. With many diseases, the secondary depression lifts when the underlying illness is treated; this is the case with hypothyroidism. In other illnesses, such as cancer, the depression itself needs to be treated, in addition to the primary disease. In general, secondary depression occurs with more serious illnesses, such as cancer, heart attack, Parkinson's disease, and stroke. Other disorders that commonly lead either directly or indirectly to secondary depression are listed on the following page.

Disorders That May Cause Depressive Symptoms

Diseases of the Nervous System:

Stroke
Dementia
Epilepsy
Fahr's disease
Huntington's disease
Hydrocephalus
Migraines
Multiple sclerosis

Narcolepsy
Parkinson's disease
Progressive
 supranuclear palsy
Sleep apnea
Trauma to the head
Tumors
Wilson's disease

Diseases Involving the Glands:

Addison's disease
Cushing's disease
Hyperaldosteronism
Menstrual disorders

Parathyroid disorders
Postpartum disorders
Thyroid disorders

Infections and Diseases of the Immune System:

AIDS
Chronic fatigue syndrome
Mononucleosis
Pneumonia
Rheumatoid arthritis
Sjogren's arteritis
Systemic lupus erythematosus
Temporal arteritis
Tuberculosis
Syphilis

Miscellaneous Disorders:

Cancer (especially pancre-
atic and other cancers of
the gastrointestinal system)
Heart disease
Lung disease
Porphyria
Kidney diseases
Vitamin deficiencies (B_{12},
C, folate, niacin, thiamine)

Drugs That May Cause Depressive Symptoms

*Drugs Used to Control Pain
or Inflammation*
Nonsteroid anti-inflammatory
agents (NSAIDs)

*Drugs Used to Treat
Heart Problems*
Alpha-methyldopa
Clonidine
Digitalis
Guanethidine
Propranolol
Reserpine
Thiazide diuretics

*Drugs Used to Treat
Nervous System Disorders*
Neuroleptic drugs
Baclofen
Benzodiazepines
Levodopa

Drugs Used to Treat Cancer
Cycloserine

Drugs Used to Treat Infection
Ethambutol
Sulfonamides
Tetracyclines

*Drugs Used to Treat Stomach
Distress*
Cimetidine
Metoclopramide
Ranitidine

Hormones
ACTH (corticotropin)
Anabolic steroids
Glucocorticoids
Oral contraceptives

Others
Amphetamines
Cocaine
Disulfiram

Drugs

Depression can also be associated with many different kinds of drugs. These include prescription medicines, over-the-counter medications, and illicit (illegal) drugs. In general, stopping the drug will end your depressive symptoms.

A word of caution: No one should stop taking a prescription drug without talking to the doctor who prescribed it, for a number of reasons. Most important, the drug could be essential to your health. Second, it isn't necessarily causing depression, which is a judgment best made by a physician. Finally, if both of you do agree to stop the medication, it may have to be done gradually, and may be replaced by another drug in the process.

Just ask your doctor.

The Good News

At first glance, the notion that your brain chemistry is just a little abnormal may not seem like very good news, much less something you're ready to share with anyone else. However, it really can be. Because there is a measurable, medical basis for depression, there are highly effective treatments that can restore your brain—and the way you feel—back to normal.

Just remember: Depression is not your fault. And it's not anyone else's fault, either. Since the way you feel or the way you act didn't create your depression, there's no reason to feel ashamed or embarrassed. And since there's nothing you've done to make the disease happen, there's nothing you alone can do—or stop doing—to make it go away. Except for one thing, if you haven't already done it.

See your doctor. *Now.*

It's Your Turn

1. Is there any history of depression in your biological family?
   - ❏ No
   - ❏ Yes   Who? _____

2. List any medications you are currently taking for any reason.

   _____

   _____

3. Are any of these medications listed on page 15?
   - ❏ No
   - ❏ Yes   Which? _____

4. Have you been diagnosed with any other general medical conditions?

   _____

   _____

   _____

5. Are any of these medical disorders on the list on page 14?
   - ❏ No
   - ❏ Yes   Which? _____

6. List any major life stresses you remember that occurred before your first episode of depression.

   _____

   _____

   _____

2

Do You Have Depression?

WHEN WE SAY we feel "depressed," we typically mean we feel sad. But many people who are sad do not have depression. And many people who have depression are not sad.

If you think that's hard to sort out, you're not alone. Doctors themselves often have a hard time telling the difference between individuals with depression and the folks in the waiting room who are temporarily just feeling "down." The same is true for the symptom of fatigue. Many people are tired because they are too stressed in their lives, or not getting enough sleep—or because they have depression. The physician may not recognize the symptoms of the disease, or may misdiagnose the fatigue or sad feelings as stemming from some other disorder. Many other persons with depression don't even make it to their doctors, blaming their symptoms on themselves rather than on an illness that they have no control over and that demands medical attention.

And some simply feel too overwhelmed to reach out for help.

Whatever the reason, the result is that depression is not diagnosed in two out of three persons who have this disease. Unrecognized depression means untreated depression. This statistic is extremely unfortunate, because depression is so treatable. Almost every depressed person can be restored to a normal or near-normal life. Without treatment, however, the picture is bad. Depression can mean months or years of mental pain and disability, and can even mean death. Sadly, 15 percent of people with this disease take their own lives.

To help make it easier to diagnose depression, the country's leading psychiatrists have come up with a list of symptoms that occur in people who have the disease. These are called the "DSM criteria," an abbreviation that refers to the book in which they are listed, namely the *Diagnostic and Statistical Manual*. The *DSM*, which is published by the American Psychiatric Association, lists the signs and symptoms of virtually every mental illness. Doctors, psychologists, social workers, and insurance companies view the *DSM* as pretty much the final word on the subject.

In the following pages, we will explore each of the *DSM* criteria for depression, one by one. Think about each description closely, and give some extra thought to the vivid personal recollections from some of the people who tell us, in their own words, of their struggles with depression. Perhaps you share some of their anguish, but never before linked it to depression.

One more point. Remember that the *DSM* is written for health care professionals to use in evaluating their patients. It is not intended for patients attempting to self-diagnose. So if you think the criteria apply to you, tell your doctor, who is qualified to make a diagnosis.

Nine Criteria for Major Depression

The Rules

According to the *DSM*, if you have at least five of the nine following symptoms, you likely have depression. These five symptoms must be present most of the day, nearly every day, for at least two weeks. Furthermore, one of those five must be either number one or number two. (This can be a little confusing, so we suggest you read this again after you have gone through the list.)

Here they are. Remember, these are not provided for you to make a self-diagnosis. Only your doctor is trained to analyze your symptoms and decide whether they fit the depression guidelines!

#1. Depressed Mood (the "Blues")

> "To me, sadness is characterized by just a general melancholy feeling about a life, a kind of sense of regret, a sense of disaffection in the life, in the absence of happiness. But depression is significantly more intense than that. It's pain, real pain."
>
> *Author William Styron*

It's deep, unremitting sadness. Everything looks gray, if not black. It's "one of those days" every day.

For some people, the "blues" might even be a slightly different color. In addition to sadness, they might feel tremendous anxiety or irritability. This is commonly the case in children and teenagers with depression. Often they tend to be overly cranky or negative, instead of appearing to be sad.

#2. Diminished Interest or Pleasure (the "Blahs")

> "I don't talk to anyone, I don't answer the phone, I just retreat. You feel that it's all over, that everything is over, that

you can't get up, you can't pretend, you can't deal with anything and you don't want to deal with anything."

Comedian Joan Rivers

Okay, so maybe you never were the life of the party, but you
still enjoyed specific activities or events in your life. Now, you just
don't care . . . about your perennial garden or your golf game,
your daughter's engagement or your upcoming vacation.

You just can't put your finger on it, but nothing is fun anymore.
Not only do you fail to take pleasure in activities that were once
enjoyable, you also can no longer recall what pleasure ever felt like.

Very often, this indifferent attitude is the first symptom to alert
the people in your life that something is drastically wrong. They
may notice it even before you do.

**Bad News,
Good News**

The inability to feel joy or pleasure actually has a name: *anhedonia*. The prefix *an* means
"without." And the word for
anything related to the ability to
experience pleasure is *hedonic*.

The bad news is that anhedonia is a very common symptom of depression. The good
news? Many experts believe that
antidepressant medications actually work best in people with
anhedonia.

#3. Weight Changes

"I also went on a diet at that time,
a really swell diet of cigarettes,
coffee, and Diet-Rite cola. I went
from 108 pounds to 73."

Actress Patty Duke

People who are depressed often experience noticeable shifts in their
weight, even when they're not deliberately trying to change their eating habits. Some people feel like
they quite literally have to force the
fork into their mouths; others can't
seem to keep the fork out.

The kind of weight loss or gain associated with depression amounts to
more than a pound or two here and
there. We're talking about a change
of more than 5 percent of your body weight in a month. If you
normally weigh 150 pounds, that means a loss to 142 pounds or a
gain to 158 pounds in thirty days. These weight fluctuations can
go on as long as depression is untreated.

#4. Sleep: Too Much or Too Little

"My mother told me I must have slept, it was impossible not to sleep in all that time, but if I slept, it was with my eyes wide open, for I had followed the green, luminous course of the second hand and the minute hand and the hour hand of the bedside clock through their circles and semicircles, every night for seven nights, without missing a second, or a minute, or an hour."

Author Sylvia Plath

Disturbed sleep goes hand in hand with depression. Some people find they can't seem to stop sleeping in the morning or throughout the day—a term we call *hypersomnia*. Others can't seem to get any sleep, which is called *insomnia*.

Insomnia wears many different faces. You may fall asleep just fine, but find yourself wide awake just a few hours later or in the

A Somatic Mystery

If you have depression, chances are you might also have a backache. Or stomach pain. Or even pain in your joints.

These are a few of the most common *somatic symptoms* of depressed people. *Somatic* is from the Greek word *somatikos*, meaning "bodily," and to doctors, somatic symptoms are various types of aches and pains, many of which bother persons with depression. The problem is that these symptoms often can't be explained. That's right—while the pain is very real, the cause of the pain may be a mystery. So even though your back may hurt, your doctor may not be able to find anything wrong with it. But if he knows that you're depressed, he'll tell you that you've experienced *somatization*. (Or, if he's a little less sensitive, he'll tell you that "it's all in your head.")

Frustrating? Yes. But once the depression is treated, these symptoms—if caused by the depression—will disappear as mysteriously as they arrived.

(Caution: Because other things can go wrong when you are depressed, don't automatically decide on your own that your headache or backache is just part of the depression. That's something your doctor should determine.)

early dawn. Or perhaps you can't get to sleep in the first place. In either case, boring books and bad TV don't get you anywhere, and you lie frustrated, watching the numbers on your clock-radio march relentlessly toward dawn.

Remember, we're talking about more than an occasional long night here or there. When you have sleep disturbances associated with depression, almost every night is a battle.

#5. Restlessness or Inactivity

"I could lie around and was glad to, sleeping or dozing sometimes twenty hours a day and in the intervals trying resolutely not to think. . . . Instead I made lists . . . hundreds of lists."

Author F. Scott Fitzgerald

Are you doing a lot of pacing, hand-wringing, or general fiddling around without accomplishing very much? That's known as *psychomotor agitation*, and it's a symptom of depression.

Or perhaps you experience a slightly different scenario. It seems to take twice as long to get anything done. In fact, you move in such slow motion that you begin to view getting dressed by noon as an accomplishment. Your speech may be slower, softer, and broken up by empty pauses.

When you have depression, these problems go well beyond the inner frustration of running around in circles that we all have now and then. Such changes in your activity level are so pronounced that even people around you can tell something is wrong.

#6. Fatigue or Loss of Energy

"I felt like I was physically tired, yet I hadn't done anything to expend energy. I really would sleep, and I'd wake up after four to five hours, go to the bathroom, and go right back to bed until ten o'clock at night."

Actress Patty Duke

One of the most common complaints people with depression have is that they feel tired all the time . . . that they just don't have the energy they used to have.

Of course, if you're not sleeping (see number four above) it's only natural that you'd feel tired. But this kind of fatigue doesn't lift with an afternoon nap. It's a constant sense of heaviness, particularly in the arms and legs, so that people feel like they are literally dragging their bodies around.

Sounding the Fatigue Alarm

In the past, doctors usually responded to a complaint of constant fatigue with a long checklist of blood tests—remember "sluggish thyroids" and "iron-poor blood"? And when these test results were found normal, patients were reassured that everything was indeed fine, and that a vitamin or a vacation would do the trick.

Except that for people with depression, vitamins and vacations aren't the solution.

Of course, problems like hypothyroidism or anemia can—and still do—cause tiredness. But now depression is one of the first things that comes to the medical mind when looking for causes of constant fatigue.

#7. Worthlessness or Guilt

"I can't figure out where to put the baby down so he's safe, so I'm holding him in one arm while I prepare to bathe him in the kitchen sink. It isn't clean. I can't find any cleanser. I want to cry. I am a terrible mother because I can't bathe the baby. I am a terrible housewife because I can't find the cleanser. I am a terrible household manager, because maybe there isn't any cleanser."

Author Kathy Cronkite

Of all the things you feel bad about, are you at the top of your list?

One of the classic symptoms of depression is an overwhelming sense of worthlessness. No matter how many accomplishments you've had, you may obsess over your past failures, dragging up long-gone work or relationship troubles to prove just how worthless you are.

You may also feel profound guilt—not because your mood and behavior have been less than wonderful, but because you can't help blowing even your smallest failings completely out of proportion. In its worst form, depression may even give you delusions that you are somehow to blame for bombings, hurricanes, or other disasters—events that occur well outside the world you really do have control over.

Some people with depression also become overly sensitive to criticism, seeing even innocent comments as evidence that their family or close friends are rejecting them.

#8. Inability to Think Clearly

"It certainly isn't that your mind goes blank. On the contrary, when you're depressed, your mind beats you to death with thoughts. It never stops. You wake up in the morning, all of the sudden you get that feeling like your head got three times heavier in one split second."

Actor Rod Steiger

Depression creates a fog that descends over your mind. Clouded by too many thoughts at once, or blurred with just one overwhelming thought, your mind is unable to function with any clarity. Thinking itself becomes a difficult task, and it's a constant struggle simply to pay attention, to remember, to make decisions.

It feels like your mind is permanently paralyzed.

Get Out Your No. 2 Pencils
Don't be alarmed if your doctor wants you to take a pop quiz about how you've been feeling. Psychiatrists and psychologists have developed a number of written tests to help doctors get information about your symptoms that you may not easily remember. Some commonly used tests include the General Health Questionnaire, the Beck Depression Inventory, the Zung Self-Rating Depression Scale, and the Hamilton Rating Scale for Depression. (By the way, these tests are merely tools, not substitutes for a good old-fashioned talk with your doctor.)

You may also be asked to take the same test later on, in order to give you and your doctor a better picture of how you're doing on your treatment for depression.

Of course, the struggle to cope with each and every decision of each and every day is frustrating and painful. If you are the rare person whose decisions don't affect other people, this internal struggle remains invisible to the outside world. However, if other individuals depend on your decisions, the results can be disastrous.

For a parent, a business executive, a teacher, a pilot, a student, the inability to think clearly can lead to family turmoil, financial setbacks, job loss, personal failure . . . or worse.

#9. Thoughts about Death

"Death by heart attack seemed particularly inviting, absolving me as it would of active responsibility, and I had toyed with the idea of self-induced pneumonia—a long, frigid, short-sleeved hike through the rainy woods."

Author William Styron

People with depression may think a lot about dying, not just as a solution to their own suffering but as a way of eliminating the misery they believe they are inflicting on their loved ones. These thoughts range from an almost wistful longing for an accident ("It would be better off for everyone if I just fell asleep at the wheel") to deliberate, even detailed, plans for committing suicide.

Even if these fantasies never turn into action, it is torture enough to be wedged between unending suffering on one hand and the frightening desire for one's own death on the other. But, as mentioned earlier, 15 percent of depressed people do eventually

Straight Talk about Suicide

There's a subtle but very widespread myth that if we talk about suicide with someone who is depressed, we're likely to give that person ideas. Nothing could be further from the truth. If you are depressed, you're quite capable of fantasizing about your death on your own. And sharing your fantasies aloud is the most critical step in making sure they don't become a reality. Furthermore, serious thoughts about suicide are a hallmark of severe depression, which requires more immediate, more intense, and additional forms of treatment than mild or moderate disease.

Make a contract with your doctor, with your spouse, or with a friend. If you feel like you are getting serious about suicide, that is, if you ever begin to put together a plan for how to do it, or have already taken steps in that direction (buying a gun, stockpiling pills, etc.), agree to let them know.

Most important, if suicide is in your thoughts, tell your doctor.

kill themselves. Because of that risk, thoughts about dying signal serious disease that demands professional help. NOW.

Exceptions to the Rules

There are several exceptions to these nine symptoms. The *DSM* says that even if you meet these criteria, you probably do *not* have depression if:

- *The symptoms are due to any general medical condition known to cause depression* (see page 14, chapter 1). Again, before diagnosing and treating depression, other underlying causes should be considered first.

- *The symptoms are due to any medication or drug known to cause depression* (see page 15, chapter 1). In this case, the most appropriate way to treat the depression is to work with your doctor to safely and sensibly discontinue the substance responsible for the problem.

- *The symptoms first appear within several months after losing a loved one.* If they do, psychiatrists believe they probably reflect the emotional and physiological upheaval that is part of the normal process of grieving. However, if they persist beyond two months, depression is a distinct possibility.

Different Types of Major Depression

The *DSM* actually divides depression into several different subtypes, based on which symptoms are involved or when episodes occur.

These distinctions give your doctor some important hints about which treatment may be most effective. *Atypical* depression, for example, may respond best to one specific type of antidepressant medication, while *melancholic* depression tends to improve on another type. *Psychotic* depression often requires additional medication in addition to antidepressant drugs.

Melancholic Depression

This severe type of depression specifically includes the inability to feel pleasure (called *anhedonia*), and agitation or loss of facial expression (called *psychomotor symptoms*). These symptoms are worse in the morning, and early morning waking is common.

Melancholic depression is most common among elderly persons and may easily be mistaken for any number of other personality changes that occur more often with aging, especially the severe loss of mental abilities known as *dementia*.

Polar Vaulting

Imagine week after week of depression. Most or all of the symptoms, most or all of the time. Then, suddenly, the fog lifts.

With a vengeance.

That's *bipolar disorder* (also known as *manic depression*), a nonstop life of ups and downs where one week you're on top of the world, and the next week you're in the depths of depression. And the "ups" are a lot more than just a really good mood. They are a frenzy of enthusiastic plans, racing thoughts, nonstop talking, and a dramatically decreased need for sleep. It is "hyper" at its most extreme, and to the outside observer, the manic depressive person can actually be quite entertaining to watch. But the manic phase is really no fun: It can be as disabling as the depressive phase, for it causes people not only to take on more daily tasks than they can handle at once, but also distracts them from completing any tasks at all. When the mania subsides, individuals are often left with the devastating consequences that unrestrained speech, shopping sprees, and sexual pursuits can have on a job, a life savings . . . or even a life.

Is bipolar depression an extreme form of depression or a completely different disorder? The answer to this remains unclear. We do know that a majority of people with bipolar disorder (about 95%) also have recurrent episodes of depression, although bipolar depression generally requires a different type of treatment.

If you want more information on manic depression, call the National Depressive and Manic-Depressive Association at 1-800-82-NDMDA (1-800-826-3632); or order literature from the American Psychiatric Association by sending them a self-addressed and stamped envelope at:

APA, Department MC 94
Division of Public Affairs
1400 K St. NW,
Washington, DC 20005

As the first treatment option for melancholic depression, experts generally believe people tend to respond better to other types of medications.

Psychotic Depression

Fifteen percent of individuals suffering from major depressive disorder also experience the effects of what we call psychotic depression. The hallmark of this type of depression is the presence of thoughts that are not in touch with the real world. For example, a person with psychosis may think of herself as wealthy, when she is not; or she may plan to have lunch with a friend who is long deceased. Such *hallucinations* or *delusions* may occur in addition to symptoms directly related to mood. For this reason, psychotic depression may be mistaken for schizophrenia. Psychotic depression tends to be recurrent, to run in families, and to evolve into bipolar depression (manic depression).

The most effective treatment for psychotic depression is antidepressant medication plus either a drug used to treat other forms of psychosis from a type of medication known as *neuroleptic drugs,* or *electroconvulsive therapy.*

Dysthymia vs. Depression

Perhaps you're familiar with *dysthymic disorder*. That's the name of another mood disorder that is somewhat similar to depression. People with dysthymia show most of the same depressive symptoms as people with major depressive disorder, making it sometimes difficult for doctors to tell the difference between the two. So what are the differences?

There are three, mainly. First, the depressed mood in dysthymic patients is present most of the time for at least *two consecutive years,* whereas bouts of depression are much shorter in length. Second, even though they last longer, the depressive symptoms of dysthymia are generally more moderate than they are in depression. And third, delusions and hallucinations—two symptoms typically found in more severe episodes of depression—are altogether absent in dysthymia.

Despite these differences, the two disorders are not completely distinct, as persons with dysthymia often develop typical depression later in their lives.

Seasonal Affective Disorder

Seasonal affective disorder (or SAD) occurs year after year during a specific season, usually winter, and disappears after the season has passed. *(Affect* is a psychiatric term for the face you present to the outside world.)

Not surprisingly, SAD tends to cluster in colder climates. It's about five times more common in New Hampshire than in Florida, although no one really knows the precise biological basis of SAD. The fact that phototherapy—exposure to ultraviolet light—seems to lift many patients out of depression suggests this problem is a mental reaction to inadequate sunlight.

An early nineteenth-century French psychiatrist named Jean-Étienne-Dominique Esquirol had an even better approach to seasonal affective disorder. The fine print on his prescriptions required patients " to be in Italy before the close of October, from whence you must not return until the month of May." Try submitting that to your insurance company.

Postpartum Depression

Almost everyone has heard of the "postpartum blues"—the episodes of crying and mood swings that occur within days after having a baby. These incidents inevitably disappear with a little time and a lot of support.

However, when you have true postpartum depression, you've got a far more serious problem than the "blues." It generally appears much later—usually around six months after you've given birth. And it involves a lot more than tears. You experience the other *DSM* symptoms of depression, not to mention the stresses of a new baby.

Postpartum depression can be treated effectively, but it still requires medical attention. It can often evolve into *bipolar depression* (see sidebar above), and there's a very good chance it will come back after the birth of another child, too. See chapter 6 for more information about postpartum depression.

Atypical Depression

After they've spent years classifying diseases into types and subtypes and subsubtypes, the medical experts are still left with a few cases that just don't fit into any type at all. Their solution has been to group all of these unique cases together into one class, which they call *atypical.*

Atypical depression tends to appear in younger people, and may be as much as three times more common in females. The two most common symptoms are overeating and oversleeping, which understandably leads to another problem, weight gain. If your depression is atypical, you may also tend to experience:

Trotula of Salerno, an eleventh-century gynecologist, once wrote the following theory on the prevalence of crying in postpartum mothers: "If the womb is too moist, the brain is filled with water, and the moisture running over to the eyes, compels them to involuntarily shed tears."

- mood reactivity, which means that you may actually cheer up (temporarily) when something positive happens in your life

- a heavy feeling in your arms or legs

- hypersensitivity to rejection by other people, which makes it difficult or impossible to sustain friendships or hold a job

- severe anxiety, in the form of intense worrying, difficulty falling asleep, or even panic and phobias

Reports and experience suggest that atypical depression is treated best by antidepressant medications.

Before We Move On

At first, finding out that all of the emotional and physical symptoms you've been experiencing add up to depression can be, well, depressing.

But think of it this way: The worst part of the nightmare is over. Once your doctor has given it a name, *depression,* you can know for sure that what you feared might be a personal weakness is in fact really just a temporary chemical weakness—a chemical weakness that can be successfully reversed with treatment.

It's Your Turn

1. Have you been feeling constantly sad or down in the dumps?
   - ❑ No
   - ❑ Yes   For how long? _____

2. Have you lost interest in the hobbies or activities that once gave you pleasure?
   - ❑ No
   - ❑ Yes   How long have you been feeling that way?_____

3. Have you lost or gained a lot of weight without deliberately trying to?
   - ❑ No
   - ❑ Yes   About how many pounds? _____

4. Do you constantly have trouble falling or staying asleep at night or trouble staying awake during the day?
   - ❑ No
   - ❑ Yes   About how long has this been going on? _____

5. Do other people remark that you can't seem to sit still or that you are moving slower than usual?
   - ❑ No
   - ❑ Yes   How long has this been going on? _____

6. Do you feel like you have no energy and are constantly dragging around?
   - ❑ No
   - ❑ Yes   How long have you felt this way? _____

7. Do you feel particularly negative or guilty about your thoughts or your actions? Do you feel you're worthless or completely responsible for the problems you see around you?
   - ❑ No
   - ❑ Yes   How long have you felt this way? _____

8. Do you have trouble paying attention? Making relatively small decisions?

❑ No

❑ Yes   How long have you noticed this? _____

9. Do you wish something would happen so that you would die? Have you thought about killing yourself or how you would do so?

❑ No

❑ Yes

10. If you answered yes to question nine, have you talked to anyone about these thoughts?

❑ Yes   Who?_____

❑ No   Stop right now and call your doctor or someone you feel close to and talk about it!

11. Count all your "yes" answers to one through nine.
How many "yes" answers did you have? _____
Did you answer "yes" to number one or number two?_____

3

Treating Depression

THESE PAGES ARE filled with good news. Really.

Very often, the hardest part of treatment is simply recognizing that your problem is, in fact, depression. Once you've done that, with a little more time, effort, and patience, you'll find that relief is usually just around the corner.

Like many other diseases, no single treatment for depression works for everyone. But that's okay, because today we have many truly effective choices on the treatment menu—mainly a variety of medications, psychotherapy, and electroconvulsive therapy.

If one approach to treatment isn't good enough, it's almost always only a matter of trying another one. And if we sound incredibly optimistic, we have good reason. Experts have performed countless studies of folks treated for depression, and their results tell us much that we like to hear.

These studies prove that we can control—and even cure—depression. They also give us a solid basis for deciding which therapies are most likely to work for which people. The clues they give us, of course, are not foolproof. Sometimes it takes a little trial and error to make the right match.

So even though your depression may leave you feeling pessimistic about your chances for help, remember this: Somewhere on that menu, there is a treatment that will work for you.

Why Treat Depression?

Left untreated, an episode of depression usually lasts for six to twelve months and then fades away. So why not just forget about treatment and simply wait it out?

The first and most obvious reason is this: Why suffer when you don't have to? A year of depression is a year that is lost both to you and to those who love you. Frankly, depression is disabling. It can jeopardize your ability to perform your job and can rob you of valuable and productive time. One study found that depressed persons take an average of eleven sick days in a ninety-day period, while the general population takes only about two days off.

More important, depression can prevent you from maintaining happy and healthy relationships. It can interfere with your ability to carry out even minor social interactions, let alone the fruitful relationships with friends or family that keep us connected to the human race—and that are essential to our overall well-being.

So depression is not only painful to you, but also to those who care about you. But treatment can save everyone a lot of pain, eliminating months and months of uncontrollable moods, emotional distress, and disruptive disability.

And There's More

eople with depression also have:

• an increased risk of dying when admitted to a nursing home

• a greater chance of getting heart disease

• poorer functioning of the immune system, which leaves them ill-equipped to fight off infection

• decreased ability to fully participate in rehabilitation following a medical illness

Another good reason to treat depression is that, like many other diseases, its early treatment can prevent a mild episode from becoming severe. Treatment also lessens the chance that depression will become a chronic (lingering) disease.

Finally, depression is a disease that can be truly dangerous to your overall health. After all, mental health is tightly intertwined with how well the rest of your body faces up to the threats of infection, bad diet, pollution, injury, and all the other challenges to life and limb you face every day. It can even be life-threatening, pushing as many as 15 percent of people with the disease to commit suicide.

Depression is not like a cold or a hangover. It is a serious disease that should be treated by a doctor. Indeed, leaving depression *untreated* is a very poor, sometimes even fatal option.

Let's Get Started

When you and your doctor agree to a treatment plan, it will probably be in one of the following forms: *medication* (pills), *psychotherapy* (conversation sessions with a specialist), the *combination* of medication and psychotherapy, or a special technique called *electroconvulsive therapy* (ECT). These are the most popular and proven weapons against depression, although there are other treatments used in special situations, such as *light therapy* for seasonal affective disorder. All of these treatment plans have both advantages and disadvantages, and some are more effective in certain patients than in others. A little later in this chapter we will discuss the various forms of treatment in greater detail.

But first, no matter which treatment you and your doctor

choose, it is important that you understand what to expect. When you first start your treatment, you should have three goals in mind:

- to reduce and eventually eliminate all symptoms of the disease as soon as possible

- to restore your ability to work, think, play, love, and feel pleasure to the level where it was before you became ill

- to lower the risk that you will experience depression again in the future

As you can see, the idea is not only to make you well, but also to keep you that way. So even though you should be feeling better in a matter of weeks after starting treatment, you should understand that treatment is a long-term process. It is divided into three stages: *acute, continuation,* and *maintenance.*

Acute Treatment

The goals of acute treatment are the same, no matter what type of treatment you choose: medication, psychotherapy, the combination of these, or ECT. These goals are (1) to greatly reduce or remove all of your depressive symptoms, and (2) to help you function the way you did before depression took control of your life.

This stage involves finding a medication that works for you, possibly making regular visits to a therapist, and keeping in close contact with your physician. You and your doctor should work out exactly how to do this, including a timetable for office visits soon after the diagnosis of depression has been made.

When your symptoms disappear with acute treatment, the disease is said to be in *remission.* But a disease in remission is not a disease that has been cured.

Yet.

Continuation Therapy

We've just said that remission is not the same thing as a cure. That's important, because stopping all treatment as soon as you

have gone into remission creates a very good chance the symptoms will soon return, even within months. That's called a *relapse.*

The second phase of treatment—the continuation phase—

Walking Away from Depression

Depressed? You might want to lace up your sneakers.

There is some evidence that mild exercise can help a person's recovery from moderate episodes of depression. Several studies show that simple workouts such as walking can actually be beneficial when added to medication or psychotherapy.

Of course, you shouldn't run out and sign up for the next marathon. The evidence for exercise as a successful treatment is still rather sketchy, and exercise might even interfere with certain types of medications. Talk to your doctor to find out if exercise is a realistic—and safe—treatment option for you. And remember, exercise is not a replacement for proven forms of treatment such as medication and psychotherapy.

focuses on keeping you in remission, preventing a relapse. After four to nine months of remission, your doctor may then taper the dosage of the antidepressant medication, while monitoring you closely for the return of any symptoms. However, even before you begin tapering the medication, symptoms sometimes recur. If they do, don't be alarmed, but be sure to inform your doctor immediately.

For some people, this phase also involves beginning psychotherapy (if it wasn't already started in the acute phase) in order to help you cope better with personal stresses as well as with the impact depression has had on your life. With or without psychotherapy, you'll be seeing your physician regularly during this time, perhaps once every one to three months.

As a general rule, if you stay in remission for six months, you have made a recovery from the original episode of depression.

Maintenance Therapy

For many people, active treatment stops with recovery. But at least half of all people who recover from one episode of depression will experience yet another episode of depression—*a recurrence*—within two years. The purpose of the maintenance phase of therapy is to prevent that from happening, especially for people who are at particular risk for a recurrence.

The maintenance phase of treatment may involve long-term antidepressant medication, particularly if you've had at least three episodes of depression or if your family or personal history suggests you may be at risk for recurrence. Follow-up visits with your physician will take place every one to three months during this phase as well.

Types of Treatment

Medication

Antidepressants—the types of drugs used to treat depression—have been around for about forty years. During that time, we've made incredible strides in our understanding of depression (like realizing that it's a disease, not a character flaw). We've also learned an amazing amount about how the chemistry of the brain relates to the chemistry of antidepressant drugs.

The result? An impressive list of medications that are not only highly effective in relieving all forms of depression, but that also can be tolerated by most people with few or no problems. And contrary to what you may have heard, antidepressant drugs are not addictive. That's true both from a chemical perspective as well as a psychological one. In fact, you won't feel any "rush" when you take an antidepressant, and it may take as long as three to four weeks of taking your medication before you feel different at all.

There are several different categories of antidepressants, but they all serve the same purpose: to increase the amount of certain substances (mainly the neurotransmitters *norepinephrine* and *serotonin*) in the brain, thus counteracting the chemical imbalance that underlies the disease. Further, all antidepressants are similar in effectiveness, and 60 to 75 percent of people respond to the first medication prescribed. For those who do not improve, a second antidepressant can be given, and half of those persons will then respond.

So what's the difference between the various antidepressants? The answer lies in which neurotransmitters they affect, and what else they affect in the brain besides neurotransmitters. It's the "what else" that often accounts for the side effects and other immense differences between the different classes of these drugs.

Before we take a closer look at the major types of antidepressants, here's a note of caution: Our comments about the drugs are only general *highlights* about the drugs, and are *by no means* complete information. If you take any one of these specific medications, you should read the accompanying drug information carefully for the most detailed and current information about your drug.

Tricyclic Antidepressants

How They Work

Although different tricyclics seem to act in different ways, they all appear to form a chemical blockade between the nerve endings in the brain and at least two neurotransmitters (norepinephrine and serotonin). The blockade interferes with the neurotransmitters' reentering the nerve cells that initially released them. Instead, the neurotransmitters remain in between the cells longer, where they remain active, tipping the chemical imbalance of depression back toward a more normal state.

> **Tricyclic Antidepressants**
> Amitriptyline
>   (Elavil, Endep)
> Desipramine
>   (Norpramin)
> Doxepin (Sinequan)
> Imipramine (Tofranil)
> Nortriptyline (Pamelor)
> Protriptyline (Vivactil)
> Trimipramine (Surmontil)
>
> Note: Clomipramine (Anafranil) is currently approved only for the treatment of obsessive compulsive disorder.

Advantages

Until better-tolerated medications were developed in the past decade, the tricyclics were the true workhorses of antidepressant therapy. They still remain highly effective for people with specific problems related to their depression. These include:

- melancholic form of depression

- insomnia related to depression, since many of the drugs in this class are sedating

- poor tolerance of other antidepressant medications

Disadvantages

While they favorably affect the brain chemistry involved in depression, the tricyclics also disrupt a number of other chemical systems that regulate various body functions. This can result in a wide range of side effects.

For example, tricyclics may cause a variety of side effects. These reactions, which are often very annoying, include:

- blurred vision

- constipation

- delirium (after high doses)

- difficulty urinating

- dry mouth

- memory trouble

- rapid heartbeat

- sedation

- sexual problems

- weight gain

While they are not life-threatening, side effects from tricyclic antidepressants can be so difficult to tolerate that many people cannot take this type of medication, even if it is effective against the depression.

Other side effects of tricyclic antidepressants are sometimes more serious, especially in the elderly. These include *orthostatic* or *postural hypotension*, which is a marked, sudden drop in the blood pressure upon standing. This drop in blood pressure can cause a feeling of extreme dizziness or even loss of consciousness, sometimes leading to falls and injuries, including broken bones. One study discovered that because of orthostatic hypotension, elderly persons taking tricyclic antidepressants actually had a higher incidence of broken hips.

Tricyclics can also alter the rhythm of the heartbeat, and therefore should not be taken by people of any age who have certain types of heart problems, especially heart block.

Another factor that contributes to side effects in older persons is that they are more likely to be taking other medications that may interact with their antidepressant drugs.

A note of caution: Abruptly stopping a tricyclic agent may cause "rebound" symptoms such as diarrhea or insomnia. Therefore, when discontinuing a tricyclic, people should do so only according to a schedule worked out by their doctors (a good rule to follow when discontinuing *any* medication).

Tetracyclics

How They Work

Like tricyclics, tetracyclic antidepressants act at the nerve endings in the brain to block uptake of norepinephrine and serotonin.

Tetracyclics
Presently, maprotiline (Ludiomil) is the only antidepressant in this class.

Advantages

The main advantage of the tetracyclics over the tricyclic antidepressants is that many of the side effects don't occur as often. Maprotiline is sedating, which actually may be a benefit when insomnia is a central feature of a person's depression.

Disadvantages

Like the tricyclics, tetracyclic antidepressants may cause anticholinergic side effects and orthostatic hypotension, and additionally may cause sedation (sleepiness) and weight gain.

A specific disadvantage to maprotiline is that it has been linked to an increased incidence of seizures.

Selective Serotonin Reuptake Inhibitors

How They Work

It's all right there in their name: These drugs inhibit (that is, slow down) the movement of the neurotransmitter serotonin back into the nerve cells in the brain (the reuptake). What sets them apart from other types of antidepressant medications is that they do so just as their name says—selectively. That means they ignore the other neurotransmitters that are also floating around at the nerve ending.

Advantages

SSRIs are so selective that they block serotonin—and only serotonin. That means they have fewer of the troublesome side effects caused by other, less selective antidepressants. This feature is particularly true with respect to certain long-term effects, like weight gain. Another advantage is that SSRIs are taken only once a day, usually in the morning. Because they are so well tolerated, SSRIs are now widely used as the first choice for most people with depression.

Some SSRIs are also being used increasingly to treat both obsessive compulsive disorder and panic disorder, and therefore may be especially beneficial when these conditions occur along with depression.

Disadvantages

Although SSRIs have fewer side effects than older types of antidepressants, unwanted reactions can occur. These tend to fall into two categories: gastrointestinal problems such as nausea, vomiting, and diarrhea; and nervous system effects such as insomnia, anxiety, and tremor. Some patients taking SSRIs also experience sexual dysfunction, which includes a loss of sexual desire.

One particularly dangerous problem with the SSRIs is that they interact with another older type of antidepressant medication known as an MAO inhibitor (see page 47). The mixture of an SSRI and an MAO inhibitor is so hazardous that one drug should not be started until the other has been totally cleared from the body.

Finally, the SSRIs may interact with a number of other drugs, including some medications used to treat heart irregularities and certain nonsedating antihistamines.

> **Selective Serotonin Reuptake Inhibitors (SSRIs)**
>
> Fluoxetine (Prozac)
> Paroxetine (Paxil)
> Sertraline (Zoloft)
>
> Note: Fluvoxamine (Luvox) is an SSRI, but is presently approved in the U.S. only for the treatment of obsessive compulsive disorder.

Newer Antidepressants

Increased research in the treatment of depression has produced novel or different agents that are effective as antidepressants. Each of the agents described below is unique or "one of a kind" in the way it works, and therefore this group is not readily broken down into specific classes of drugs.

Trazodone (Desyrel)

How It Works

Trazodone is a weak blocker of sertonin reuptake.

Advantages

Because this drug has a sedative effect, it may be advantageous when insomnia or anxiety is a prominent part of the depression.

Disadvantages

Sedation may be an unwanted side effect when anxiety isn't a problem. It can also cause headaches, GI upset, and orthostatic hypotension. A unique side effect is *priapism,* a painful, persistent erection in males. Irregular heartbeats and *edema* (swelling in the legs), although very rare, can occur.

Newer Antidepressants
Trazodone (Desyrel)
Venlafaxine (Effexor)
Mirtazapine (Remeron)
Nefazodone (Serzone)
Bupropion (Wellbutrin)

Venlafaxine (Effexor)

How It Works

Because of its unique chemical structure, venlafaxine is unlike any of the other antidepressants. It acts by inhibiting the reuptake of serotonin and norepinephrine, and is a weak inhibitor of dopamine reuptake.

Advantages

Unlike the tricyclics, venlafaxine is associated with fewer side effects, making it another effective option for initial antidepressant therapy. Some evidence suggests that Venlafaxine acts more quickly than other antidepressants, and it may be more effective in severely depressed patients, especially those requiring hospitalization. Another practical advantage of venlafaxine is that it can be taken once a day, typically in the morning. It also appears to interact with other medications less often than other antidepressants.

Disadvantages

Nausea seems to be the most common side effect, and even when it occurs, nausea usually disappears quickly. Venlafaxine may also cause anxiety, insomnia, dizziness, headache, constipation, sweating, loss of appetite, and difficulty attaining orgasm and ejaculation. Blood pressure rises in a very small percentage (about 5 percent) of people taking venlafaxine at higher doses, so it's important to closely monitor the blood pressure while taking this medication. Like the SSRIs, the interaction between venlafaxine and MAO inhibitors is potentially fatal, so it is essential to leave time for the MAO inhibitor to clear out of the body before beginning venlafaxine.

Mirtazapine (Remeron)

How It Works

Mirtazapine is different from many other antidepressants. It blocks a specific type of serotonin receptor and increases the activity of neurotransmitter systems.

Advantages

It is taken once per day, and has a relatively low incidence of anticholinergic effects. Because it is sedating, it can be useful in persons with insomnia. Sexual dysfunction is less common than with the SSRIs.

Disadvantages

Sleepiness is common, which may impair thinking and motor skills, such as driving a car. Dizziness and weight gain due to increased appetite may occur. It should not be taken within two weeks after receiving an MAO inhibitor.

The dose should be reduced in the elderly and in patients with liver and kidney impairment.

Nefazodone (Serzone)

How It Works

Nefazodone is structurally related to trazodone and blocks the uptake of serotonin and, to a lesser extent, norepinephrine.

Advantages

Sexual dysfunction is not a significant problem, as has been reported with other antidepressants. Sedation and orthostatic hypotension are less likely to occur compared to its other cousin, trazodone. It may be safer than other antidepressants in patients with heart disease.

Disadvantages

Nefazodone must be taken twice per day, compared to many of the other newer antidepressants that need to be taken only once per day. Headache, sleepiness, dry mouth, nausea, dizziness, insomnia, and constipation all have been reported in more than 10 percent of people taking the drug. It should also not be taken within fourteen days of taking an MAO inhibitor and can also interact with some medications that are used to treat hay fever or anxiety.

Bupropion (Wellbutrin)

How It Works

Bupropion is a newer type of antidepressant drug that became available at about the same time that the SSRIs were introduced. Although we don't know how exactly bupropion works, there is evidence that it blocks norepinephrine and dopamine. We also know that it's unique among antidepressants in that it doesn't directly block the activity of serotonin.

Advantages

Bupropion is generally a well-tolerated antidepressant. Its side effects are relatively mild, and include nervousness and insomnia. Some patients also experience nausea, vomiting, diarrhea, and headaches. Because bupropion does not cause sexual dysfunction, it is a good alternative to SSRIs when sexual problems occur. It has also proven a good choice for many elderly patients.

Disadvantages

It must be taken two or three times a day, and when taken in very high doses (above the recommended range), bupropion may cause seizures. Even recommended doses of Bupropion can cause seizures in individuals who have an increased risk of seizures from conditions such as epilepsy, bulimia, anorexia nervosa, brain tumor, or head trauma.

Monoamine Oxidase Inhibitors

How They Work

Neurotransmitters are normally broken down in the body by an enzyme called *monoamine oxidase* (MAO). MAO inhibitors inactivate this enzyme, leaving a greater amount of neurotransmitter—including norepineph-rine, serotonin, or dopamine, depending on the drug.

MAO Inhibitors
Isocarboxazid (Marplan)
Phenelzine (Nardil)
Tranylcypromine (Parnate

Advantages

MAO inhibitors may be particularly effective for persons with:

- atypical depression, a special form of the disease whose symptoms include overeating, excessive sleeping, sensitivity to rejection by others, a sense of paralysis, anxiety, or increased sensitivity to changes in the environment

- failure to improve after trials of therapy with tricyclic and tettracyclic antidepressants

- a history of already proven responsiveness to MAO inhibitors, or family members with depression who have been successfully treated with these drugs

Disadvantages

When an MAO inhibitor interacts with a substance known as *tyramine*, the result can be an episode of severe high blood pressure, or even a potentially fatal stroke or heart attack. Unfortunately, tyramine is present in many foods and drinks, including a large number of those that have been aged or fermented (such as cheese and wine), pickled or smoked, or contaminated by bacteria. People who take MAO inhibitors must carefully avoid a long list of cough, cold, and allergy preparations, as well as prescription drugs like meperidine (Demerol). Epinephrine, which is commonly used

Some foods containing tyramine:

Aged cheese	Raisins
Alcohol (especially beer and wine)	Sour cream
Avocado	Soy sauce
Fava beans	Summer sausage
Pickled or smoked meat	Yogurt
Plums (very ripe)	

with a local anesthetic in dental work, should be avoided as well. Therefore it's very important that persons taking MAO inhibitors inform their doctors and dentists, and further, carefully read all food and medication labels.

And again, MAO inhibitors can be extremely dangerous when combined with other antidepressants, such as SSRIs and venlafaxine.

Other Medications Used in Depression

Under certain circumstances, two other types of medication may be prescribed for people with depression: *anxiolytics* (also known as antianxiety drugs) and *lithium.*

Anxiolytics

In general, antianxiety drugs are not very effective in the treatment of depression itself. In addition, the potential for addiction to anxiolytic drugs has long troubled the medical community, and many people experience severe withdrawal symptoms when they stop taking anxiolytics after using them for prolonged periods of time. They may also experience a phenomenon known as "rebounding," which means that the symptoms return with even greater force once the drug has been discontinued.

> **Anxiolytics**
> Alprazolam (Xanax)
> Buspirone (BuSpar)
> Chlordiazepoxide
>   (Librelease, Libritabs)
> Diazepam (Valium)

Nevertheless, anxiolytics may be a practical alternative for people with medical conditions that make it impossible for them to take any true antidepressant drug. Alprazolam appears to have the best record of this class of medications in treating depression, although it has been studied only in the acute phase of treatment. Further studies are necessary to see whether its addictive potential would complicate use of the drug over longer periods of time.

Lithium

Lithium has been used for several decades to treat people with bipolar depression (manic depression), a specialized form of depression distinguished by intense swings between depressed and manic moods (see chapter 1). Lithium is a naturally occurring salt-like substance that has long been very effective in smoothing out

St. John's What?

It may be a weed, but for many people it's also a remedy for depression.

St. John's wort is a yellow blossoming herb that for centuries Europeans—espe cially Germans—have brewed in their tea as a cure for various ailments. But mor recently the *wort* (old English for "plant") has received serious attention as a treat ment option for depression.

Officially, St. John's wort is known as *Hypericum perforatum*, and a recent stud suggests that it might be as effective as synthetic (man-made) antidepressants ir treating milder forms of depression. Interestingly, we do not know exactly hov the little herb works. What we do know is that St. John's wort seems to have a healthy effect on neurotransmitter activity in the brain, much like synthetic anti depressants. St. John's wort also seems to cause fewer, maybe even milder, sid effects, and costs less to purchase than typical antidepressant drugs. It's not surpris ing that in Germany, where *Johanniswort* is widely approved and easily available the herbal remedy is four times more popular than prescription antidepressants.

But before you plant a Johnny garden or move to Germany, pay attention to a few warnings. First, scientific studies of St. John's wort are incomplete. They have not yet determined if St. John's wort can remain effective (or safe) over long pe riods of time, nor is there evidence for its effectiveness against *severe* episodes o depression. In addition, the effectiveness of the herb has not been compared tc that of the newer class of antidepressants, such as the SSRIs.

Second, there are some side effects. Doctors have reported dizziness, skin rash dry mouth, stomachache, and fatigue, while ranchers have reported that cow who graze on the herb are extrasensitive to sunlight. And because the available re search is incomplete, doctors presently advise against the use of St. John's wort b children and pregnant women. Combining St. John's wort with another antide pressant is also not recommended, as it could lead to complications from an over load of serotonin in the brain.

The best advice for anyone interested in St. John's wort is to wait just a little longer. There is so much interest in this wonder weed that studies are currentl underway, and their results will be made available soon. Stay in touch with reli able medical news and ask your doctor to keep you informed.

the ups and downs of bipolar depression, although no one really knows exactly how it does so. Lithium has recently been used in addition to antidepressant drugs in people whose depression is not improving with one drug alone. Adding a second drug to existing treatment, a strategy known as *augmentation,* may help anywhere from 20 to 50 percent of depressed people who have failed to get better with a single antidepressant agent.

The most common side effects of lithium are drowsiness, weight gain, nausea, diarrhea, skin rash, and swelling of the arms and legs. These problems tend to be mild and usually disappear in a short time. Other reactions such as excessive thirst, hand tremor, and increased urination may last awhile longer.

The major drawback of lithium is that once it enters the bloodstream, there is a very fine line between the amount that improves symptoms and the amount that causes potentially serious side effects, such as seizures and coma. That line narrows even more when dehydration occurs, brought on by fever, diarrhea, and even excessive sweating. People who take lithium must therefore have their blood sampled regularly in order to make sure that the drug is not reaching potentially toxic levels, and they must be especially careful to avoid dehydration.

> ## Lithium: A Periodically Correct Element
> Remember the periodic table of the elements? Sure you do. It's the list of naturally occurring chemicals, their abbreviations, and their atomic weights that you had to memorize in high school chemistry. Lithium is right there beneath "H" (hydrogen) and to the left of "Be" (beryllium). Not such a useless table after all, is it?

Choosing an Antidepressant Agent

If all these antidepressants work so well, how do we choose the right one?

The truth is that when all factors are considered, there is usually not a clear, purely scientific basis for selecting one of the newer antidepressant agents over another. Only a trial at the right dose for a period of time will tell whether a particular drug is right for you. Luckily, many different medications can work just as well in the same person.

Nevertheless, choosing an antidepressant involves a number of important considerations. Here are the kinds of things that doctors think about when selecting a specific drug:

- What are the drug's short-term side effects? Some people are more prone to certain side effects.

- What side effects are likely to last throughout the treatment? This is an important consideration when determining the practicality of maintenance therapy.

- If a specific antidepressant has been taken before, did it help? And did you tolerate the side effects? If a drug has worked in the past, there's a good chance it will work again.

- If the drug hasn't worked for you before, there's a good chance it won't work now. Make sure you tell your doctor about medications that you know you've had problems with in the past. This will save you both time and money in the course of your treatment.

- If any first-degree relatives have tried a particular drug, did it work for them? Remember, depression runs in many families. There is evidence that the way people respond to a particular antidepressant class may actually be a sort of family trait.

- Do you have any other medical conditions that would make a particular drug's side effects truly dangerous? For example, an antidepressant that may raise blood pressure or disturb the heart rhythm should not be given to a person with hypertension, a history of stroke, or a heart condition.

- Are you taking other medications that are known to cause conflicts with the antidepressant? Drug combinations can be a tricky business—one drug may cause another to become ineffective, or the interaction between the two could be potentially toxic.

The most important component of this rather complex equation, of course, is you. Under the careful guidance of your doctor, the final decision is yours. This decision requires you to understand all the alternatives at your disposal, as well as the pros and cons of each, before you start taking an antidepressant (or any other medication, for that matter). And remember, no one is ever obligated to take any medication.

Medication or Psychotherapy?

The United States Department of Health and Human Services asked this same question of a panel of experts in the diagnosis and treatment of depression. Here's what the panel advised:

IF YOU HAVE . . .	THEN YOU HAVE . . .	AND YOU SHOULD FIRST TRY . . .
some symptoms of depression and it's a little hard to do the things you need to do	mild depression	medication *or* psychotherapy
many symptoms of depression and it's often impossible to do the things you need to do	moderate depression	medication *with or without* psychotherapy
Nearly all of the symptoms of depression and it's always impossible to do the things you need to do	severe depression	medication *with or without* psychotherapy

The Department of Health recommends psychotherapy *alone* only in more mild forms of depression. In addition, it generally recommends a combined treatment of medication and psychotherapy for patients who have not completely responded to either treatment alone, or for patients who have had a longer, more complicated history of depression. It advises, however, that the combination of medication and psychotherapy does not necessarily provide any unique advantage in uncomplicated forms of depression.

So what's the best advice? Think these things over carefully and share your concerns with your doctor right from the start. The wisest decisions are made together.

Psychotherapy

Psychotherapy is a general term for the many different techniques used by psychiatrists, psychologists, and social workers to treat emotional problems. Because depression is a disease that cuts a path right through your emotional well-being, psychotherapy can play an important role in its treatment and may be recommended for you at some point after the diagnosis is made.

Rules of the Psychotherapy Road

If you are considering psychotherapy, here are some guidelines to keep in mind:

1. Consider psychotherapy *instead* of medication only if your depression is mild to moderate. In other cases, the experts recommend it as a useful, but optional, addition to medication.

2. Make sure your therapist has experience in working with persons with depression. If you are uncertain about a therapist's qualifications, it is best to rely on your personal physician's recommendations. You can also call a major organization dedicated to mental health for a listing of therapists in your area (see the appendix for a list to get you started). Then, make sure you feel comfortable with that person as your partner in treatment. If you don't feel comfortable, be honest about your feelings with the therapist and, if necessary, find someone else.

3. Allow your therapist to focus first on strategies for lifting the symptoms of depression rather than on overhauling your personality. (That's another issue entirely and can come later if it's something you really want to explore further.)

4. Ask your doctor and therapist at the very beginning of psychotherapy when you can expect your symptoms of depression to improve. After that period of time elapses, tell them if you are not feeling better. Many patients believe that they'll disappoint their doctors by telling them that they haven't improved,

Jne Phone Call

¯hat's how close you are to finding a highly respected organization dedicated to ¯he well-being of persons with depression (as well as other mental illnesses) and ¯heir families. Since 1979, the National Alliance for the Mentally Ill (NAMI) has Ͻrovided support, education, advocacy, and research; its resources include Ͻrochures and fact sheets, a catalogue of books and audiotapes, and newsletters ϲontaining practical tips as well as scientific and legislative news.

One of the most valuable services NAMI provides is a network of over a thouϛand local and state affiliates. That means it can put you in touch with people ϱnd services right in your area—including psychotherapists with good track ϸecords in helping people with depression.

ϛtart by contacting the national headquarters at:

The National Alliance for the Mentally Ill
200 North Glebe Road, Suite 1015
Arlington, VA 22203-3754
Toll-free help-line: 1-800-950-NAMI
Telephone: 703-524-7600
E-mail: NAMIofc@AOL.com

so they may say that they feel fine when they really don't. Don't do this! Be honest about your progress or lack of progress. In general, six weeks of therapy should bring about noticeable improvement. Lack of improvement in that time is a pretty reliable sign that you may need an antidepressant medication in addition to—or in place of—psychotherapy.

5. Be prepared to make a reasonable commitment to your therapy sessions. A visit at least once a week is a good schedule for psychotherapy.

Kinds of Therapy

Scan the self-help shelf in any bookstore and you'll get a good idea of just how many different types of psychotherapies there are. A few years ago, someone with a lot of time on his hands actually counted them, and came up with over 250 different forms of psychotherapy.

Now the federal government doesn't demand that we study the effectiveness of a particular psychotherapy like it does for a drug before someone can use it in people with depression. However, studies that have focused on the major types of psychotherapies suggest that, when administered properly, their effectiveness is generally similar to medications.

Certain types of psychotherapy are rapidly gaining ground in the treatment of depression because they work in comparatively short periods of time and with the specific goal of alleviating symptoms of the disease.

While many psychotherapists follow one school rather strictly, others may borrow freely from any strategy that they believe will work for an individual patient.

Let's look a little closer at these schools: *cognitive* therapy, *interpersonal* therapy, *brief dynamic* psychotherapy, and *behavioral* therapy.

Therapist ABCs

• A *psychiatrist* is a physician (MD or DO) whose specialty is the diagnosis and treatment of mental disorders.

• A *clinical psychologist* has a doctoral degree (usually a Ph.D.) in psychology and training in counseling, therapy, and psychological testing. A psychologist cannot prescribe drugs but is likely to know a lot about antidepressant medications.

• A *social worker* has a master's degree in social work (MSW) and specialized training in counseling. A social worker cannot prescribe medication, but may be familiar with antidepressant medications.

Remember, the string of letters that follows a therapist's name does not guarantee expertise in treating depression.

Cognitive Therapy

The word "cognition" refers to thoughts. And cognitive therapy aims to change your way of thinking. When cognitive therapy is applied to depression, it helps to break the pattern of negative thinking that distorts how people with this disease view the world.

Cognitive therapy first helps persons with depression recognize how they constantly focus on the negative aspects of themselves, their world, and their future. It helps these individuals see that they are looking at life through gray-colored glasses.

The next step is to help the individual make the connection between this continual pessimism and gloomy feelings. After all, who wouldn't be depressed if all he or she saw was gray?

Finally, cognitive therapy helps people replace their "doom and gloom" perspectives with positive alternatives. This is accomplished by teaching specific methods for making optimistic thinking a permanent part of their mentality. The key steps identifying the negative thoughts and challenging them are what make cognitive therapy effective and not simply a process of "thinking happy thoughts."

Interpersonal Therapy

One of the hallmarks of depression is that relationships with family and friends become a lot less meaningful and a lot more stressful. It's no surprise that difficulty in getting along with people closest to us inevitably makes depression worse.

Interpersonal psychotherapy is designed to help resolve some of these difficulties. It stresses ways to improve how we communicate and associate with other people. Very often, spouses or other family members will be asked to participate in some therapy sessions, when appropriate.

Brief Dynamic Psychotherapy

This form of therapy concentrates on the inner workings of the unconscious mind—specifically, conflicts in an individual's personality that may make him or her especially vulnerable to a psychological problem (in this case, depression).

But the key word here is *brief.*

A person entering brief dynamic psychotherapy first makes a contract with the therapist that treatment will end after a certain number of sessions, usually twelve to twenty meetings over three to six months. The sessions focus on one specific problem—for example, a continual inability to leave a terrible job—and look to improve the situation by identifying the deeper, underlying issues that have given rise to the problem at hand.

Brief dynamic psychotherapy is usually not appropriate for severely depressed people. These patients have symptoms that may prevent them from becoming truly involved in the therapeutic process, and so they would require much more time than this type of treatment allows.

Behavior Therapy

Unlike other "talk therapies," behavior therapy focuses on action. Simply stated, its guiding principle is that the shortest path to healthy behavior is to address the inappropriate behavior itself, rather than to examine the underlying reasons that make us act in various unhealthy ways. When behavior therapy is used to treat depression, the doctor focuses less on the patient's inner conflicts and troubled feelings and more on specific techniques for scheduling activities, attaining self-control, improving social skills, or solving problems. These techniques are learned in a session with the therapist and then practiced again and again out in the real world. (That means homework.)

Studies of behavior therapy suggest it may be among the more effective approaches for people with depression.

Other Forms of Therapy

In addition to psychotherapy, there are many other forms of non-medical treatment, including *marital* therapy, *electroconvulsive* therapy and *light* therapy.

Marital Therapy

Depression can harm marriages and other intimate relationships. But the reverse is also true: Bad relationships can bring about depression, especially in people who are prone to depression in the first place.

Consider these facts. In half of all marriages considered "distressed," either the husband or the wife (or both) suffers from depression. A marital conflict often comes right before an episode of depression, and before relapses or recurrences as well. And in many cases, marital friction lingers even after the depression has lifted, which seeds the potential for yet another depressive episode.

So is depression the marital chicken or the egg? Answering that question is one of the most complex tasks facing the psychotherapist treating a person with depression. To get the job done right, it's necessary to work with both parties. Depressed people who are in troubled intimate relationships (and you certainly don't have to be married to have problems with a significant other) should consider marital counseling in addition to medication or individual psychotherapy. Marital therapy itself may be based on a number of different approaches, including behavior therapy and/or cognitive therapy.

Electroconvulsive Therapy

To many people, "shock therapy" epitomizes a twentieth-century version of the tortures that passed for treatment of mental illness in medieval Europe.

Nothing could be further from the truth. In fact, for a very select number of people with severe depression, electroconvulsive therapy—or ECT—is often the only treatment that works.

Because ECT is a procedure that requires anesthesia, the decision to undergo ECT must be a cautious one, made not only with your regular doctor but with a psychiatrist as well.

How It Works

ECT sends a brief electrical current through the brain, triggering a seizure. This seizure in turn has a balancing effect on several neurotransmitters in the brain.

It's completely understandable if you're feeling a few qualms about allowing electricity into your brain. But fortunately, the procedure is nothing like what you've seen in *The Bride of Frankenstein,* and it's not even like the traumatic procedure you may remember from *One Flew Over the Cuckoo's Nest.* ECT is done under anesthesia (most often, via medicine that drips into a vein in your hand) and with a muscle relaxant (so that your body remains loose and flexible). The entire procedure takes only ten minutes or so. There are no sudden jolts, no violent jerks. In fact, to a person watching from the outside, a person receiving ECT doesn't appear much different from any other patient lying on a hospital bed.

Advantages

ECT may be the answer if:

- several different classes of antidepressant drugs have failed to work

- the side effects of antidepressant drugs have been so great or potentially risky that they cannot be used safely

- depressive symptoms are so severe that a rapid response is necessary, e.g., the individual is suicidal or in a virtually vegetative state

- the depression is complicated by other psychotic disorders

Disadvantages

The disadvantages of ECT include:

- short-term memory loss (usually for the events occurring immediately before and after treatment)

- the medical risks that are part of any procedure involving general anesthesia

- costs of hospitalization

- the need to follow up with antidepressant medication, even if the procedure works very well

In addition, ECT is not a treatment option if you also have certain other medical conditions, such as lesions in the brain or a recent heart attack.

Light Therapy

Light therapy currently remains on the unofficial list of treatments for depression because it's not entirely clear whether it helps depression over time.

Light therapy is reserved for individuals suffering from seasonal affective disorder (SAD), a type of depression that typically strikes in the winter and lifts by spring or summer (see chapter 2, page 31). Many people believe SAD represents a biological cry for more daylight, and that's why the treatment involves exposure to light.

But don't bother sitting under your reading lamp. Light therapy involves rays known as *broad-spectrum light,* transmitted through special boxes or visors. If you're interested in light therapy, be sure to see an expert in this highly specialized field.

Sometimes a Hospital Helps

No matter what the illness, the trend in medical practice over the past several years has been to hospitalize fewer people and to keep the number of days spent in the hospital to a minimum.

The same forces are at work in the treatment of mental illness, including depression. Fortunately, in the great majority of instances, depression can be well treated with medication and psychotherapy administered through a program of regular outpatient visits. However, from time to time, people need the type of medical care that only hospitals can provide. For example, a hospital may be the best (or only) way to quickly remove a person who lives alone from surroundings that may escalate the chances of suicide. Hospitalization may also be necessary to care for a person who has had a toxic reaction to an antidepressant drug.

It's true for people with skin conditions, with heart disease, or with cancer, and it's true for people with depression: sometimes a hospital helps.

It's Your Turn

1. Which of the following best describes your most recent episode of depression?

❑ *Mild* (some symptoms that made it a little hard to complete activities)

❑ *Moderate* (many symptoms that often made it impossible to complete activities)

❑ *Severe* (nearly all symptoms and always impossible to complete activities)

2. A. Have you taken any antidepressant medications in the past?
❑ Yes
❑ No
If so, what is the name of the medication?_____

B. Did this antidepressant medication help your depression?
❑ Yes
❑ No

C. Did this antidepressant drug cause any side effects?
❑ Yes
❑ No
If so, which side effects did you experience? _____

Did these side effects decrease after you took the medication for a while?
❑ Yes
❑ No

3. A. Have any of your biological relatives taken any antidepressant medications in the past?
❑ Yes
❑ No
If so, what was the name of the medication (or medications)?_____

B. Did this medication help your relative's depression?
- ❑ Yes
- ❑ No

C. Did it cause any troublesome side effects?
- ❑ Yes
- ❑ No

4. Do you have any other medical conditions?
- ❑ Yes
- ❑ No

If so, what?

_____

5. Are you taking any other medications?
- ❑ Yes
- ❑ No

If so, what? _____

Have you told the doctor who is treating your depression that you are taking this medication?
- ❑ Yes
- ❑ No

6. Has your doctor recommended psychotherapy for you?
- ❑ Yes
- ❑ No

If so, what kind?_____

7. A. Has your doctor recommended that you spend some time in the hospital?
- ❑ Yes
- ❑ No

B. Even if your doctor hasn't mentioned it, do you believe you should be hospitalized?
- ❑ Yes
- ❑ No

C. If so, why do you think you should be hospitalized?

_____

_____

D. Have you discussed your desire to be hospitalized with your doctor?

❏   Yes

❏   No

4

What Can You Do
for Depression?

IF YOU HAD any other type of illness, you would feel happy that effective treatment could be in sight. But depression, by its very nature, has a way of dampening such feelings of optimism. In fact, depressive symptoms such as feeling worthless or not feeling pleasure may rob you of any interest in even attempting to return to your former, positive self.

Just trust us. With a little effort on your part, help, and a return to a life worth living, are on the way.

This chapter is devoted to that little effort, explaining what *you* can do to help conquer depression. As you read, keep in mind that it's these little things that can make the biggest difference.

Take Your Medicine

If you have depression, the first thing you can do for yourself is to take the antidepressant medication your doctor prescribes for you.

"But I don't need to take drugs. They're just a crutch."

You may not want to take antidepressant medication because, after all, you should be able to lick the problem yourself. Right?

Wrong. That attitude comes from the old " weakness of will" mentality. While this reaction is a natural and completely understandable response to antidepressant drug treatment, you need only to remind yourself that depression is a disease caused by chemical changes in the brain. Therefore, use of a chemical to correct those changes isn't a "crutch," but rather, as Mike Wallace says in this book's foreword, it's merely the nourishment your brain needs to resume its normal activity.

"I'm not a 'druggie.' I don't need to run away from my problems."

It's good that you aren't craving substances to help you escape from reality. But don't worry, that's not what these drugs do. Antidepressants do not get you high. In fact, most people find that when it's working properly, an antidepressant drug makes them feel more like themselves, because normal chemical balance in the brain is being restored. No self-respecting junkie would be caught within a thousand yards of a drug that did that. In fact, as proof that antidepressant drugs have virtually no "street" value, did you know that they can be prescribed without a special permit—called a DEA number—that the government does demand for such ordinary, but potentially addicting, drugs as some sleeping pills or muscle relaxants?

So let's set the record straight:

• Antidepressants are medicines designed to correct the chemical imbalance in your brain that gives rise to a set of symptoms known as depression.

• Antidepressant medications are not recreational drugs that alter your mind.

• Antidepressants will not significantly, if at all, dull your senses or impair your mental or physical functioning. And even though they cause some side effects, most occur at the beginning of treatment and don't last long after that.

• Antidepressants are not addictive. When your doctor tells you it's time to stop taking your medication, you will find it easy to do so. And if he wants you to stay on the medication for longer than usual, it is okay. Studies show that antidepressants arc safe even when taken over long periods of time.

In short, antidepressants are scientifically proven to be both safe and effective. They play the same role in the treatment of disease as insulin does in diabetes, thyroid hormone does in thyroid deficiency, and iron does in anemia. In all instances, the body's own chemicals are merely being restored or put back in balance.

Believe us: you can believe in your antidepressant. But you must be certain to take it just as your doctor advises.

Be Involved

When you're depressed, your first inclination may be to draw the sheets up over your head or to crawl into a closet and stay there. And certainly the last thing you feel like doing is getting involved with anybody or anything.

But please, please, pull back the sheets, crack open that door, and get involved with your treatment.

What exactly do we mean by getting involved? It starts by asking your doctor all those questions that you need answered. How quickly will you see improvement with a specific treatment? What are the risks? What kind of side effects can you expect and how long do they usually last? What does it cost?

Being involved may also require learning about depression on your own. Just be sure you are careful about who is doing the teaching. You've made a great start, of course, by reading *Ask the Doctor!* Other good sources of information are available from your doctor and from the major organizations that we've listed in the appendix.

Graduate with Honors

It makes perfect sense: The best way to graduate from depression is to first become a student.

It's true. Educating yourself and your family about depression is perhaps the greatest thing you can do for your treatment. Studies have actually shown that patients who learn and understand their disease recover more quickly and completely than patients who don't. In fact, the U.S. Department of Health and Human Services includes in their *Clinical Practice Guidelines* the following conclusion: "A depressed outpatient's adherence to treatment can be improved by educating the patient and, in many cases, the family about the treatment, its potential side effects, and its likelihood of success."

This means that knowing all there is to know about depression will make easier to recover. You'll be more likely to go along with the doctor's orders if you know why he's given them in the first place. So be sure to ask a lot of questions and be willing to learn!

Being involved also means following the treatment exactly as your doctor has laid it out for you. You will need to take your medication, attend group and individual therapy when it has been advised, and make changes in your day-to-day life that your doctor suggests.

All this sounds fairly obvious until you realize that *compliance*—the term for following treatment instructions—is easy to talk about, but often difficult to do. That's true for anyone on any kind of treatment program, but especially so if you are depressed, because the disease makes everything an effort. In fact, failure to follow treatment directions is common enough to have its own name—

you guessed it, *noncompliance*. While it may reflect anything from occasional forgetfulness to downright defiance, noncompliance seriously jeopardizes your chances of getting better.

Your Compliance Checklist

- Take your medication as instructed.

- Avoid any foods or other medications (including other nonprescription preparations) that may interfere with your medication. You should also stay away from foods or drugs that have a depressing effect in their own right (see chapter 3). Ask your doctor or pharmacist for a list of these foods and drugs.

- Call your doctor if you experience any side effects. Do not adjust the dose of your medication yourself, as this could possibly cause some dangerous reactions, or at least prevent the drug from helping as much as it could.

- Schedule follow-up visits with your doctor as instructed and be sure to keep the appointment!

- If you receive psychotherapy, keep your appointments with your therapist. Likewise, be sure to complete any assignments he gives you.

Finally, being involved with treatment means staying honest with the people who are caring for you. In a well-meaning effort to please their physicians or therapists, some patients may say they are feeling better when they are really not improving at all. True, your caregivers want therapy to work. But in order to make that happen, they need to know the truth. And only you can give them that. So if you're not improving, say so.

Therapists want—and *need*—to know if you are unhappy with the interaction between the two of you or with the direction your therapy is taking. Doctors also want—and *need*—to know if you are having any side effects from your medication and whether or not you can handle them.

And before stopping any treatment that doesn't seem to be working, every physician needs to be made aware if something else—such as "recreational" drug use or an unfilled prescription—is complicating the picture.

Be Patient, Be Realistic

Depression has been described as living within a smoke-filled mind. Even when you pop the window open, it takes some time for the air to clear.

It's the same with medication and psychotherapy, which open the window to your emotions. It takes time to restore balance among the chemicals in your brain and for the fresh air of a healthy neurotransmitter system to clear your mind of the symptoms that have been smothering you. So we encourage you to be patient, and know that with time, the air will clear.

And keep your expectations realistic. If a particular treatment is going to work for you, it will realistically take at least six weeks for you to feel genuine improvement in your mood, sleep, and other depressive symptoms. The improvement will continue over the next several weeks, and within a few months you could very well be functioning like your old self. Of course, everyone is different, and it could take less—or more—time for healing to take place.

While we're on the subject of realistic expectations, keep in mind that you and your doctor may not find the right solution right away. In about half of all patients, the first antidepressant drug works. But because no firm scientific guidelines are available to match specific drugs to specific patients, finding the right antidepressant often involves a bit of trial and error. So don't be alarmed if your doctor seems to be experimenting with the dosage of your medication or even switching you to another drug after several weeks.

If after six weeks your symptoms are still there, don't worry. Your doctor has several more effective options that the two of you can try. These options include replacing your medication with another, adding a second medication to work together with the first one, and adding psychotherapy.

Talk Back to Depression

One of the most crippling symptoms of depression is the inability to think clearly. Indeed, it often makes people with depression believe that it's them against the world rather than them against their own chemical imbalance.

One way to keep your world in the right perspective is to talk back to the disease when it starts making too much noise within your mind. Here are a few thoughts you might want to hurl back:

- The negative way you perceive life right now is how the disease is making you feel. Tell yourself: *My depression is making me feel this way about myself. (No, I'm not a total failure at my job, fatter than anyone else I know, or the worst mother in the school.)*

- Depression is a disease. You didn't make yourself depressed and neither did your parents, your spouse, or your children. And, as we've been saying all along, you aren't depressed because of any weakness in your character. Tell yourself: *I have a disease, and my treatment will make it better in time.*

- Sheer willpower will not force your depression to disappear. Seeking medical help is a sign of your personal courage, and you should congratulate yourself for that. Tell yourself: *No, I'm not crazy because I'm seeing a doctor for depression. My disease needs to be treated by a doctor, who treats many forms of neurological diseases.*

- You will not feel this way forever or, for that matter, for much longer. When your treatment begins to work, your symptoms will start to disappear. *(I'm so sick and tired of feeling sick and tired every morning.)* Keep reminding yourself: *Just a little more time on treatment, and then the pain will start to go away.*

Keep Your Goals Bite-Sized

When you recover from the flu, you don't expect to bound out of bed and run a marathon the first day the aching, cough, and fever are gone. Healing takes time.

So it goes as you recover from depression. Instead of scolding yourself for what you don't feel up to doing (and we all know that blaming yourself is common in depression), each day establish a series of limited, very specific activities that you can do. Always set realistic goals that are within the reach of your current frame of mind. For example, if you haven't been able to work through the afternoon because of fatigue, try working a half day for a while.

Try the same approach for activities outside of work, like household chores or recreation. You may not have the energy to mow the lawn, but you may find that cutting some flowers might be just right, for now. Or you can hit a tennis ball or practice your serve rather than taking on a three-set match.

And, if it's all you can do at the moment, just take a walk to the mailbox and back. It's okay—even therapeutic—to push yourself, as long as you are gentle and kind to yourself in the process.

Bite-sized goals like these serve three purposes. First, they give you some needed feeling of accomplishment. Second, they serve as a helpful yardstick for measuring your improvement. And finally, by giving you specific activities to focus on, they keep you from getting caught in the endless cycle of boredom that often traps people with depression.

One other piece of advice. Wherever possible, avoid making decisions that affect your life in a big way. If circumstances force a major life decision upon you, share your dilemma and explore its possible solutions with your spouse, a good friend whom you really trust, or your doctor before you take action. And remember: Most decisions in life can just wait.

R_X: Mop and Pail

Difficulty concentrating is a classic symptom of depression. If that's true for you, set goals that don't require a lot of mental energy. It's probably not a good time to balance your checkbook. But it is a fine time to get lost in purely physical chores—especially those that you may have neglected. You'll appreciate the sense of accomplishment, not to mention the smell of a clean refrigerator, the sight of a weeded garden, or the feel of a well groomed family pet.

Watch What Goes in Your Mouth

Because alcohol itself depresses the brain, it may contribute to depression, making symptoms much more noticeable and difficult to treat. Consider staying away from beer, wine, and other forms of liquor entirely, or, at the very least, drink with *strict* moderation.

You might also want to gradually cut back on caffeine. Because it's a stimulant, caffeine can worsen depressive symptoms such as anxiety, nervousness, psychomotor agitation, and insomnia. But be careful not to stop your caffeine intake too quickly, especially if it's a big part of your diet: Caffeine withdrawal can also cause depressive symptoms.

Caffeine Culprits

The average American consumes about 200 mg of caffeine each day. Here are some of the more common sources of caffeine:

- one cup of coffee (brewed) = 120 mg

- one cup of coffee (instant) = 78 mg

- one cup of tea = 48 mg

- one can of caffeinated soda = 45 mg

- cold medicine (one tablet) = 25–50 mg

- one chocolate candy bar = 5 mg

What about medication that you take, either regularly or when you experience a particular problem? Over-the-counter drugs are not harmless. Many contain chemicals that can interfere with antidepressant medications. Be certain your doctor is aware of all medications—prescription and nonprescription—that you take regularly or that you might take under special circumstances, such as for a cold or an upset stomach. And always read the labels for extra safety.

Get Some Sleep

Sleep is an important remedy for both your body and your mind to aid the healing from any disease, including depression. A good night's sleep, every night, is a *must.*

But what are you supposed to do when it's the depression that's keeping you awake in the first place? A good place to start is to pay close attention to your usual bedtime habits. The experts suggest that you stick to a sleep routine as much as possible. That means getting into bed at the same time every night and getting out of bed at the same time every morning. And if possible, you should also try to make your daytime activities into a routine. So if you walk your dog at six o'clock one night, walk him at six *every* night, and so on. All of this regularity, even if it is not particularly exciting, helps establish regular body rhythms, which are key to good sleep patterns.

Again, cut down on the caffeine. The stimulating effects of coffee or chocolate or a Coke can last up to eight hours, so avoid foods like these after midday.

If you exercise, the experts suggest you do it in the afternoon or evening—but not right before bedtime. Exercise warms the body, and it's the cooling down period afterward that often makes people drowsy. If you don't exercise, it's not a problem: A warm bath can have the same sleep-inducing effect.

Once you are in bed, make sure not only that your pillows and sheets are comfortable, but also that the room temperature is appropriate. Doctors say that a cooler room will help you fall asleep, so the thermostat should be set lower than most of us are accustomed to, maybe sixty-four to sixty-eight degrees. Next, avoid watching the clock; you may need to hide it out of sight if you find yourself staring. And you might not want to watch the TV before bedtime either: Thirty minutes of violent crimes on the evening news is not the best possible prelude to a night of sweet dreams. In fact, doctors suggest that you not do anything in bed except sleep. If you're reading, working, or watching TV in bed, you aren't asleep! So try not to associate the bed with anything except *sleeping.*

What about sleeping pills, or a "nightcap" of wine or another form of alcohol at bedtime?

While sleep-inducing drugs or alcohol may blanket you with the drowsiness you need to drift off to sleep, they ultimately can make matters worse. First of all, they may alter the natural patterns of genuine, restful sleep. You may think you're sleeping, but your body's sleep center knows it isn't getting the biological rest it needs. And so it refuses to reward you with the mental energy and control you need to get through the next day.

Second, if you have depression, medicating yourself to sleep may actually worsen the disease, since many of these substances

Pillow Trivia

If counting sheep doesn't make you tired, try some of these numbers . . .

- The average American adult gets about 7.5 hours of sleep each night.

- Experts believe that about sixty million American adults suffer from some form of insomnia—that's *one* in *three*.

- One study concluded that Americans today sleep 20 percent *less* than Americans did one hundred years ago.

- The U.S. Department of Transportation calculates that sleepy drivers cause two hundred thousand car accidents each year.

- A 1991 Gallup study concluded that people with insomnia had more than twice as many car accidents as people who got a good night's sleep.

are themselves known to create chemical imbalances in the brain. The result can be to act against the effects of your antidepressant medication and everything else you are doing to overcome this disease.

Our best advice is to make your sleep disturbances a priority-one discussion with your doctor—especially if you think a sleep medication may be necessary.

Maybe Get Some Exercise

By this time, everyone knows that exercise provides measurable medical benefits for many conditions, from high blood pressure to pregnancy to heart attacks. But did you know that some research tells us that exercise might also have an antidepressant effect?

It's true. A regular program of aerobic exercise has helped many people with depression feel and function better than they did before they started working out. In one study, even a regular bodybuilding routine significantly decreased symptoms of depression.

Even though you may not feel like moving a muscle, try giving yourself an extra push—to the gym, pool, or park. You don't have to make it a passion; in fact, it's best if you keep your activities light. A few laps in the pool or a brisk walk around the block is just fine. Anything that works those muscles for at least several minutes of sustained exercise is worth a try, so long as your doctor approves.

Don't Go It Alone

Those who have recovered from depression often credit their success, at least in part, to a spouse, a friend, a coworker—anyone who supported them and encouraged them during the time of their illness. And most of these people were supportive despite requests not to be: Depressed patients often prefer to go it alone, even though it's best that they don't.

Look around you. If you can see beyond your feelings of worthlessness and guilt caused by the disease, you're sure to see family and friends waiting for you on the other side. It may take a bit of education on their part, especially if they are not familiar with depression as a disease. (For a start, you might ask them to read parts of *Ask the Doctor*.) When they learn the facts, they will begin to appreciate how you feel, and they may then provide invaluable support to you.

You may also find that it's helpful to interact with other people who themselves have successfully coped with depression. There are a number of associations that offer support groups and publications. And for that growing number of computer buffs, there are informal newsgroups on the Internet. See the appendix on page 105 for a list of resources.

It's Your Turn

1. About Drug Therapy

If you are taking an antidepressant drug, what is it called?

_____

How long have you been taking it?

_____

What has been the first positive change that you've noticed?

_____

Have you experienced any side effects?

_____

2. About Psychotherapy

If you are participating in psychotherapy, how often do you see your therapist?

_____

How long did he or she expect it to take for you to feel less depressed?

_____

3. How much alcohol do you drink weekly?

_____

4. Think back to last week. If you had a good sleep any night, what activity directly preceded falling asleep?

_____

5. What type of exercise are you getting on a regular basis?

_____

6. List three people you could consider reaching out to as "support system" as you begin to recover from depression.

_____

_____

_____

5

How Are
You Doing?

WE ALL LOVE to watch crowds. Sitting on a park bench, or in the bleachers in a football stadium, or in the front seat of a car traveling through town, we like to look at other people.

As we watch all those other folks, one thing is clear: Everyone looks different than everyone else. And the reason we all *look* different is because we *are* different.

Therein lies a warning for this chapter—as well as much else we have to say about depression throughout *Ask the Doctor.* Because we're all different, we respond to treatment in different ways as well.

That's why what follows are only *general* guidelines of what you can expect. If you aren't feeling like your former, happy self six weeks into treatment, it might be that your body is just taking longer to respond to the medication than the " average" person's body does.

The same is true for sleep, energy level, and eating. We are all different, indeed.

It's Just a Matter of Time

On average, it takes about six weeks for antidepressant medications to make a noticeable difference in your symptoms. But don't let that mislead you.

As antidepressant drugs take on the remarkable task of balancing your brain chemistry, the first changes take place within days. So, while major improvement in symptoms may take longer, you could notice some subtle, but good, changes in the way you feel much sooner than that.

Such as . . .

Sleeping Better

The first change you'll probably notice is that you are sleeping better. Gradually you will find yourself falling asleep with greater ease, sleeping longer and longer, and, eventually, feeling much more rested when you wake up. These effects prove that antidepressant drugs are very different from sleeping pills, which often leave you with a distinctive "hangover" the next morning.

Eating Better, Too

Right around the same time that your sleeping habits begin to improve, you may notice your normal appetite slowly returning.

Food tastes like it used to, and meals are no longer an ordeal. If depression caused you to overeat, you should be able to control your food choices and quantities instead of letting them control you.

Antidepressant drugs themselves can cause weight changes, especially the older tricyclic antidepressants, which cause weight gain.

Renewed Energy and Concentration

Feeling like you have a little more get up and go? Are the little things on your " to do" list just a little easier to start and complete? These changes are all the benefits of "de-depressing" your brain.

Giving your body better nutrition and sleep can help with your overall energy level, too. These changes may be so gradual that other people may actually notice a new kick in your step before you do. And while you may not confuse the slow renewal of energy with any sort of new zest for life, it can make a surprising difference in your ability to work, attend school, and simply get on with the chores of daily living.

And Then, a Mood You Can Live With

Pretty ironic, isn't it? The very symptom of depression that most people find the most devastating—the sad, bleak, or negative mood—is typically the last symptom to disappear.

However, after about six weeks of effective treatment on an antidepressant medication, you should feel the darkness itself beginning to lift. It won't take many more weeks before you feel like your old self again.

A Word about Side Effects

Some wise old scientist (probably one who never got sick) once said that the side effects of a medication sometimes are needed to prove that it is working. That observation may be reassuring to scientists, but it doesn't offer much comfort for patients who wonder if the cure is worth it.

Fortunately, the newer antidepressant medications used most commonly today are remarkably free of dangerous or truly troubling side effects. When you get your prescription, be sure to ask your pharmacist or doctor about any reactions you should watch out for, including any that require an immediate phone call to the office. In most states, this information is available from the pharmacist in an easy-to-understand pamphlet. If you don't receive such material when you pick up your prescription, ask for it. And then be sure to read it! (Reminder: Chapter 3 contains information about the most common side effects of specific antidepressant drugs.)

In general, the side effects of most antidepressant drugs—particularly the newer ones—are mild, occur at the beginning of treatment, and typically disappear after a few weeks. So if you experience any problems with side effects, give yourself some time to

Prunes, Anyone?

Here are a few tips to help you manage some of the more common minor, but annoying, side effects of antidepressant medication:

Dry mouth: Drink lots of water, chew gum, suck on hard candy, brush your teeth frequently, and if nothing else helps, ask your doctor or pharmacist about artificial saliva preparations.

Constipation: Try some natural laxatives such as bran cereals, prunes, and fruit.

Nausea: Since nausea occurs immediately after taking the medication, ask your doctor if the pill can be taken at bedtime.

Drowsiness: Ask your doctor if you can take the pill at bedtime.

Dizziness: Remember to stand slowly when you get out of bed or out of a chair.

Sex problems: Tell your doctor, because he may not ask. There are a variety of reasons why sex problems may occur, including antidepressant drugs themselves. And the solution depends on the cause.

adjust. Chances are, you will find these reactions merely a nuisance and well worth the price of feeling better.

However, if you find the problems persist or are really too difficult to tolerate, call your doctor. Very often, a small adjustment in the dose will be all that is necessary. If not, talk with your doctor about the pros and cons of switching to another drug.

Don't Stop Now

Eighty percent of people with depression will find an effective treatment. So chances are extremely good that you'll be feeling better soon. But if you stop taking your medicine just when you're beginning to feel better, you'll be tipping the scales in the wrong direction . . . toward a relapse of your original episode or a recurrence of another one.

In general, you'll probably need to continue your medication for at least several months. And even that is an estimate, one that depends on how many episodes of depression you've had in the past, how long they've lasted, and how severe they have been. If you've already suffered three episodes of depression, for example, your doctor may want you to consider prolonged, perhaps even lifelong, therapy.

If you and your doctor have determined that it is the right time to discontinue treatment, remember that stopping " cold turkey" isn't a good idea. Teaching your body to withdraw from any medication is a chemically delicate process, so follow your doctor's specific instructions for slowly tapering off the medication.

It's also not a good idea to think about discontinuing treatment when you are in the middle of a personal crisis. That lessens the chances of long-term success.

Get a Handle on Stress

Just when you are in the midst of recovery, the IRS may call; or your daughter may elope with a wrestler; or your boss may catch you playing solitaire on the company computer. Bingo! Instant stress.

For many people, stressful experiences increase the risk of another episode of depression. And, as wonderful as antidepressants are, you may need help in learning how to better cope with life's unexpected changes. This is an invaluable role of psycho-therapy, which helps you to:

- develop effective strategies for coping with stress

- deal with any problems your depression has caused in your relationships

- create a supportive social network if you tend to live a more isolated lifestyle

Another word about psychotherapy. While we of course do not advocate contracting depression as a means for improving your life, some people find that, in the long-run this illness results in a better life. Why? Because depression forces you to look at the way you live and the way you respond to the people and events around you. Through psychotherapy, you may emerge from this ordeal better equipped not only to cope, but to thrive in this complex, challenging world.

Develop an Early-Warning System

An ounce of prevention is better than a ton of cure.

That is why it's a good idea to do as much as you can to minimize the stresses in your life. In the end, however, there are always things about life we can't change. Whatever coping strategies you use, you will likely encounter trying times from those pesky "circumstances beyond your control."

Whether you run into a minor crisis or a major loss, it is crucial to be sensitive to any changes in how you are feeling and how you see the world. How's your sleep? How are your eating habits? If the physical or emotional symptoms of depression start to feel continuous and all too familiar, let your doctor know. Developing an early-warning system is an effective way of heading off another episode of depression.

It's Your Turn

Here's a completely informal and unscientific way to chart your progress.

1. First, think back to your very worst moments—when you were truly in the pits of the disease.

Now, compare them to how you've been feeling after at least three weeks of treatment, and circle the single most appropriate number below. (If you haven't started treatment yet, come back again in three weeks!)

	Worse		About the Same		Much Better	
A sense of sadness	0	1	2	3	4	5
Inability to enjoy pleasurable activities	0	1	2	3	4	5
Appetite/weight changes	0	1	2	3	4	5
Sleep disturbances	0	1	2	3	4	5
Restlessness/ inactivity	0	1	2	3	4	5
Fatigue or loss of energy	0	1	2	3	4	5
Worthlessness or guilt	0	1	2	3	4	5
Inability to think clearly	0	1	2	3	4	5
Thoughts about death	0	1	2	3	4	5

2. It should now be six weeks later, that is, nine weeks after you first started treatment. Once again, think back to your very worst moments of depression. Compare them to how you are feeling now.

	Worse			About the Same		Much Better
A sense of sadness	0	1	2	3	4	5
Inability to enjoy pleasurable activities	0	1	2	3	4	5
Appetite/weight changes	0	1	2	3	4	5
Sleep disturbances	0	1	2	3	4	5
Restlessness/ inactivity	0	1	2	3	4	5
Fatigue or loss of energy	0	1	2	3	4	5
Worthlessness or guilt	0	1	2	3	4	5
Inability to think clearly	0	1	2	3	4	5
Thoughts about death	0	1	2	3	4	5

6

Special Folks,
Special Conditions

As you have learned by now, just about anyone can develop depression. Regardless of who, what, or where you are, depression can suddenly become a part—a miserable part—of your life.

While we've spent five chapters trying to explain what can be done about this common problem, all the rules don't apply to all the players. There are still people whose problems are sometimes so unique that they deserve special mention.

This chapter is for them.

Special Folks

Children and Teenagers

It's only been about two decades since the medical world turned its attention to depression in children and adolescents. While that may seem like a long time, it means that the little girls and boys in the first studies are still just young adults right now. So we're only beginning to get a picture of what having the disease as a child means over the course of a lifetime.

Here's what we *do* know:

- Depression occurs in about 2 percent of school-age children and in over 4 percent of teenagers.

- Children of parents with depression are at higher risk of developing the disease.

- When a person experiences a first episode of depression before age twenty, it tends to be a recurring problem throughout adulthood.

- In general, the younger the child, the more severe the problem.

Symptoms in Children

In general, the symptoms of depression are pretty much the same as they are in adults, although it can be more difficult to recognize them. After all, you can't expect your seven-year-old to tell you that he's been experiencing a lack of pleasure lately!

Teenage Girls and Depression

Prior to puberty, depression occurs in just about as many boys as girls. After puberty, however, girls are two to three times more likely than boys to have depression.

One classic symptom of depression in children is irritability, that is, becoming short-tempered or cranky at the slightest irritation. An inability to concentrate for very long is also common. Another sign is the presence of *somatic symptoms,* which we discussed in chapter 2. Mysterious, recurring stomachaches, for example, may be a clue to underlying depression.

Eventually, these symptoms take their toll on schoolwork, and a bad report card can actually be the first sign of depression. Refusal to go to school is common in depressed children.

If You Suspect Your Child Is Depressed . . .

Every child can be " cranky" at times, for a lot of reasons other than depression. The same thing is true for kids who can't focus on their homework, remember where they left their sneakers, or get on the school bus without one last desperate whine about a tummy ache. That sort of behavior is usually just part of being a child.

The trick is to figure out (1) whether troublesome behavior represents a *change* from the child's usual behavior, and (2) whether it has been going on for too long. And that's a trick best left in the hands of pediatricians or specialists in adolescent medicine. They have been trained to ask kids special questions in just the right way and to conduct physical examinations that will pinpoint whether any other health problem like depression may be lurking beneath the surface.

Of course, it's only natural that you would try to cheer up a sad child. However, if the problem is not a bad mood but a mood disorder like depression, your struggles will ultimately prove useless. The problem of childhood depression is compounded if there are difficulties at school. Being labeled by peers or by teachers as a "problem" at school can give your child a poor self-image that can be difficult to erase, even if the depression itself is successfully treated.

What should you do? If your child's behavior has changed dramatically, or if you have any other reason to suspect depression, get your pediatrician involved immediately.

Seniors

While there can be many losses connected with getting older, aging itself is not a cause of depression.

When depression does occur in older persons, it should be

given serious attention. Depression can complicate other illnesses that older people more often have, such as heart disease and stroke. And most important, people age sixty-five and older commit suicide more than any other age group, with depression being the most common cause.

The good news is that depression can be treated just as effectively in seniors as in everyone else. The not-so-good news is that spotting depression in older folks is sometimes difficult to do. In fact, half of the people with depression in this age group are not aware that they have this disease. Even though the symptoms of depression are basically the same in people of all ages, in elderly people the signs of depression are frequently overlooked.

Why? First, seniors are more likely to have other illnesses, which means that they're also more likely to be on some kind of medication. And as we learned in chapter 1, several diseases and medications themselves create symptoms of depression. Unfortunately, doctors often think they're looking at a normal symptom of some other disease, or side effect from a certain medication, when they're really looking at a person with depression.

Another reason why depression is often overlooked in seniors is that we sometimes just *expect* the elderly to act moody and sad because it's likely they've experienced more loss—loss of family, financial security, and independence. Many seniors themselves assume that their depressive symptoms are a normal part of aging, and so they withhold from complaining to their families or doctor. Further, when seniors with depression *do* complain, it tends to be more about *somatic symptoms*—that is, body aches and pains—rather than about changes in their mood, difficulty sleeping, or feeling guilty. And because seniors generally live less active lifestyles, visiting the doctor is sometimes an exciting change in routine—so much so that depressed moods are temporarily replaced by happiness about getting out of the house. All of these factors can mislead doctors into thinking that something other than depression is distressing their patients, often resulting in costly, unnecessary tests and treatments.

Fortunately there are ways to "test" older people to help determine if they're suffering from depression. In addition to the exams we mentioned in chapter 2, such as the Hamilton Rating Scale for Depression and the Beck Depression Inventory, there is also a test designed especially for seniors: the Geriatric Depression

Scale. This test is not only effective, but also efficient. It consists of only fifteen simple questions and generally takes only five or so minutes to complete.

The Cost of Undiagnosed Depression

Undetected (and untreated) depression in the elderly takes an immense personal and economic toll. Elderly people with undiagnosed depression:

- seek out health care services more frequently

- stay in the hospital longer

- find it more difficult to comply with medical treatments

- suffer more complications from other medical illnesses, and are more likely to die from these diseases

- face a higher risk of suicide

Treatment Works

Once depression is diagnosed in older individuals, there is just a minor difference in how antidepressant medication is pre- scribed. Because our metabolism slows down with aging, it takes a smaller amount of a drug to get the job done in older persons. For the same reason, it also takes a smaller dose of a drug to trigger a side effect. So, in general, dosages of antidepressant medication tend to be lower in elderly people. Once again, because older individuals may have other medical diseases or may be taking other drugs that could interact with the antidepressant, it's essential that they remain in close contact with their doctors.

Seniors should also be aware of certain important side effects. For example, a fall in blood pressure in the upright position (called *orthostatic hypotension*) is common in the elderly, and is also caused by certain antidepressants, especially some of the older tricyclic drugs. The SSRIs are safe in this regard. All of the tricyclic drugs can also worsen various types of heart electrical problems, which also occur more frequently in the elderly.

Psychotherapy may also help depressed seniors deal with the difficulties that often go hand in hand with growing old: loss of loved ones, isolation from family and friends, and changes in financial and/or physical well-being.

Special Conditions

Grief

Grief is a normal reaction to the loss of a loved one, and is a state of mind that shares many of the symptoms of depression: sadness, loss of pleasure, a change in sleeping and eating habits, loss of energy, inability to concentrate, and physical slowness. But unlike depression, grief is generally expressed without feelings of profound guilt, psychotic behavior, or active thoughts of suicide.

And, unlike depression, grief is healthy. As a normal reaction, it moves us over a period of time toward recovery from our loss. A person who experiences these symptoms for a few months after a death of a close family member or friend is experiencing normal grief and requires only compassion and support. But a person who experiences these symptoms for longer periods, and every day for most of each day, is likely suffering from depression and probably requires medical attention.

If depression complicates grief, antidepressant medication and sometimes psychotherapy may be necessary, just as with any other person with depression.

Postpartum Depression

Sure, a baby is the most wonderful gift a mother can imagine. New mothers sometimes cry the moment they first hold their baby. But if they still cry more than two weeks after delivery, those are probably not tears of joy.

When Grief Triggers Depression

Certain people may be at higher risk of developing depression following the death of a loved one. They include grieving individuals who also:

- have a personal or family history of the disease unrelated to anyone else's death

- have active thoughts about suicide

- are in poor health

- are unhappy with their jobs

Postpartum depression is a type of depression that occurs in mothers any time from two weeks to one year after giving birth. (The word "postpartum" means "after childbirth.") The most common time is at about six months.

It is an entirely different—and more severe—problem than "postpartum blues," which consist of brief episodes of crying and fragile moods that occur in as many as 80 percent of women one to five days after delivery. The blues is a problem that reflects, at least in part, the completely natural hormonal hurricane a woman experiences in moving from pregnancy to motherhood.

The difference between the blues and depression? With a little reassurance and time, postpartum blues disappear on their own. Postpartum depression does not.

Symptoms of Postpartum Depression

Women with postpartum depression often feel very anxious or even panic-stricken. They are unable to summon much interest in their new baby. The disease causes early-morning insomnia and, at its worst, confusion or even hallucinations about the child.

Obviously, these symptoms interfere with a developing healthy bond between the mother and her baby. When postpartum depression is severe, the mother's disinterest or delusions about the child may even threaten the baby's well-being. Tragically, women can experience so much guilt over these feelings that they work overtime to keep these " shameful" symptoms hidden from everyone around them. That makes it hard for them to get the help that they—and their babies—deserve.

Treatment for Postpartum Depression

Like all other forms of depression, postpartum depression is a disease that can be treated effectively with medication, psychotherapy, or a combination of both. However, there are certain medications that breast-feeding mothers should avoid, so it's important for women to let doctors know if they plan to breast-feed *before* starting any medication. In addition, experience suggests that electroconvulsive therapy might be especially helpful in treating women who've had recurring episodes of postpartum depression.

In all cases of postpartum depression, the obstetrician or family physician should be able to provide immediate help, or can refer the mother to a specialist for treatment.

Eating Disorders

Depression is often a part of eating disorders, which we read and hear a lot about these days. People with *anorexia* generally eat only enough to keep their body weight over the bare minimum that's necessary to survive. People with *bulimia,* in contrast, consume large amounts of food, but afterward vomit or use laxatives in a frantic effort to rid their bodies of the calories they just consumed.

We've known for a while now that anorexia, bulimia, and other eating disorders are especially prevalent in girls and young women. Here's something else that's come to light: Where there are eating disorders, depression is not far away. Studies have shown that up to three out of four persons with eating disorders have had depression at some point in their lives. Thirty to fifty percent of people suffering from an eating disorder have depression *at the same time.*

Severe lack of nourishment (an adequate number of calories and the right amount of essential vitamins and minerals) itself can cause symptoms of depression. After all, like any machine, a body deprived of fuel can't function properly, if at all. For that reason, doctors will generally treat the eating disorder first. If symptoms of depression linger once the individual is eating properly, the depression can be treated with antidepressant medication and psychotherapy.

Because Once Is Enough
If a woman has had postpartum depression in the past, chances are fifty-fifty that it will happen again with the next child. This possibility should be discussed with the obstetrician during pregnancy—or even before, if practical—so that plans can be made to prevent it from recurring, or at least to treat it in the earliest stages if it does recur.

Substance Abuse

It is not uncommon for substance abusers to be depressed, especially because alcohol and many drugs of abuse themselves create chemical imbalances in the brain that in turn cause symptoms of depression. In many cases, the process of withdrawal from drugs such as cocaine and amphetamines (speed) also causes depressive symptoms.

It is important to realize that substance abuse is not simply a way people who are depressed handle their problems. In fact, studies show that depression usually does not lead to alcoholism. Both alcoholism and addiction to prescription or street drugs are medical disorders, separate and distinct from depression. However, it is not uncommon for alcoholics to eventually develop a full episode of depression. The advice from the experts who study substance abuse is to treat the addiction first. If symptoms of depression remain even after the person has been "clean" for several months, specific antidepressant treatment may be necessary.

Other Conditions

Depression sometimes occurs along with other types of mental disorders. These include anxiety, panic, phobic, personality, and obsessive compulsive disorders. Therefore treatment for these disorders should also include a careful search for evidence of depression. A physician trained in mental disorders can decide whether it's better to treat multiple conditions simultaneously or to focus on just one. Very often, treating only the depression or the other disorder will suffice to control both.

Phone numbers for support organizations that specialize in anxiety, panic, phobic, personality, and obsessive compulsive disorders are included in the appendix.

It's Your Turn

1. If you're a parent . . .
   Does your child or teenager seem especially irritable lately?
   ❑ No
   ❑ Yes

   Have you received any reports of behavioral problems in school?
   ❑ No
   ❑ Yes

3. For mothers: Have you experienced prolonged sadness or anxiety when your baby was anywhere from two months to one year old?
   ❑ No
   ❑ Yes

4. If you are currently pregnant and you've answered "yes" to the previous question, have you spoken to your obstetrician about postpartum depression?
   ❑ No
   ❑ Yes

5. If you are over sixty-five and are feeling depressed . . .
   What other illnesses do you have at present?

   _____

   _____

   What other medications are you taking at present?

   _____

   _____

6. Do you make yourself vomit after eating or use laxatives regularly?
   ❑ No
   ❑ Yes

7. Has anyone talked with you about the possibility that you may have an eating disorder?
   - ❏ No
   - ❏ Yes

8. If you've recently suffered the death of a close family member or friend . . .
   How long ago? _____

Are you experiencing any symptoms of depression (see pages 21–27 for a list of these symptoms)?
   - ❏ No
   - ❏ Yes

9. Do you regularly use alcohol, prescription medications, or street drugs?
   - ❏ No
   - ❏ Yes

7

Depression FAQs (Frequently Asked Questions)

What's the difference between sadness and depression?

Sadness is a *feeling* that we all have at times. It is a mood that we can usually shake off, given a change in circumstances, a sunny day, or often just with a little time.

Depression is a *disease* that involves many other symptoms, often in addition to sadness. And like other diseases, you can't shake off true depression, no matter how hard you try.

So how can you tell if you have depression?

See your doctor. He will ask you a lot of questions to find out if you have the right combination of symptoms that qualify for a diagnosis of depression. Questions about your sleeping and eating habits, your energy levels, your ability to focus. You'll also be given a physical exam and perhaps a blood test or two to make sure there are no other medical problems causing your symptoms.

What causes depression?

Several things play a role. The primary problem is a chemical imbalance in the brain that centers around abnormally low levels of a specialized chemical known as serotonin. No one really knows what causes serotonin levels in the brain affected by depression to drop, but we do know that your genetic makeup and the occurrence of certain types of stressful events in your life play an important role in getting the disease. Depression may also be caused by certain medical conditions and can even be a side effect of many prescription or over-the-counter medications.

Can anyone get depression?

Yes. And millions do. About 15 percent of Americans, most between ages twenty and fifty. But it's definitely an equal-opportunity disease: Depression occurs in all age groups (including children, teenagers, and the elderly), without any higher incidence in any particular racial or economic group. Women are twice as likely to get depression as men are.

If other people in your family have had depression, will you?

Your chances are higher, but it's not a certainty. If one of your first-degree relatives (parents, sibling, or immediate offspring) has depression, you're about three times more likely to develop depression than someone with no family history of depression. Medical scientists believe that what gets passed along through genes is actually a vulnerability for getting the disease, and that it takes specific types of events (such as stress) in a person's life to turn this vulnerability into an actual episode of the disease.

Does depression ever go away by itself?

A single episode of depression will usually last about six to twelve months, and if left untreated, it usually goes away by itself. However, untreated depression often returns. If you've had one bout with depression, there's a 50 percent chance you'll experience a second episode. If you've had two episodes, there's a 70 percent chance it will return a third time. And if you've had three episodes of depression, you're facing a 90 percent chance of the disease recurring again.

Is the treatment for depression specific for this disease?

Yes. We now have several entire classes of medications specifically designed to treat depression. And they get the job done in eight out of ten people with depression.

What happens if an antidepressant drug doesn't work for you?

Depending on the reason, you can move on to another choice on the long list of drugs that are proven to be effective in treating depression. Keep in mind that an antidepressant drug that works well for one person may not be the answer for another. And because there's no real way to predict which drug will be ideal for a given individual, it may take a little trial and error before you and your doctor find the right answer for you.

Will antidepressant drugs make you feel drugged?

The newer antidepressant agents very seldom have this effect. And while some people may feel a little drowsy when they first start taking some of the older antidepressant drugs (especially the tricyclic class of medications), this feeling usually disappears as the body gets used to the medication.

Can you become addicted to antidepressant medication?

No. Antidepressant medications are nothing like the "mind-altering" drugs sold on the street. Here are two critical facts about drugs used in the treatment of depression: First, they don't make you high or otherwise alter your mind. Second, they are not addictive. Therefore, when you and your doctor think the time is right, you'll be able to stop antidepressant drug therapy with no ill effects, although gradual tapering may be necessary for reasons unrelated to "dependence."

Do you have to take antidepressant medication forever?

Usually not. It takes about six weeks of treatment for the first symptoms to go away and a little longer for you to feel like your old self. Depending on the number, the duration, and the severity of the episodes of depression you've had in the past, your doctor may want to continue treatment long enough to minimize the chance of a relapse. In general, prolonged and even lifelong antidepressant treatment is usually reserved for people who have already had three or more episodes of depression.

What is the role of psychotherapy?

Although psychotherapy takes many forms, it may be used initially for persons with mild or moderate depression. One of the main reasons for using psychotherapy as opposed to medication is simply patient preference; many people are opposed to medications in any form, for any reason.

When psychotherapy is chosen, what can it accomplish?

Some of the objectives of psychotherapy in persons with mild or moderate depression are to:

- remove symptoms

- restore normal function to daily life

- prevent a recurrence of depression

- help in correcting problems brought about by the depression, such as marital (and other family) discord and occupational conflicts

- improve compliance with medication

What are the disadvantages of psychotherapy?

Psychotherapy can be very beneficial to many people. But it does have drawbacks. They include the following:

- The value of psychotherapy in severe depression has not been proven.

- Many patients fail to follow through with their scheduled visits or the "homework" assigned to them.

- There are many forms of psychotherapy, and not all have been proven effective.

- Not all persons with depression respond.

- Some psychotherapists are better than others.

- Therapy sessions take time, may be inconvenient, and may be expensive.

- Treatment effects generally take longer than medication.

What about combined medication and psychotherapy?

This is not usually recommended routinely for the initial treatment of most patients, but some circumstances seem to warrant both medication and psychotherapy together. These include:

- when either treatment by itself is only partly successful

- when two very different problems need to be addressed, such as depression and serious marital discord

- when the depression is chronic, with periods of poor recovery between episodes

Appendix:
Resources for Depression and Manic Depression, and Related Organizations

American Foundation for Suicide Prevention (AFSP)
120 Wall Street, 22nd Floor
New York, NY 10005
(212) 363-3500
1-888-333-2377
Web site: http://www.afsp.org

The AFSP is a nonprofit organization that specializes in supporting research for suicide prevention and the treatment of depression. The toll-free number accesses support for survivors, as well as education and support information for persons at risk.

American Psychiatric Association
1400 K Street, N.W.
Washington, D.C. 20005
(202) 682-6220

The friendly staff of the American Psychiatric Association provides helpful brochures on a number of issues related to mood disorders, including depression, anxiety disorders, phobias, eating disorders, and substance abuse. The brochures are free of charge, and can be obtained by writing or calling the association.

American Psychological Association
750 First Street, N.E.
Washington, D.C. 20002-4242
(202) 336-5500

For free pamphlets and brochures on a variety of mood disorders, write to the address above.

The Depression and Related Affective Disorders Association (DRADA)
Meyer 3-181, 600 North Wolfe Street
Baltimore, MD 21287-7381
(410) 955-4647
Web site: http://infonet.welch.jhu.edu/departments/drada/default

DRADA provides education and information, mutual self-help support groups, peer support, and research support for persons and family members troubled by affective disorders such as depression and manic depression. A nonprofit organization, DRADA works in cooperation with the Department of Psychiatry at Johns Hopkins University to ensure the quality of their programs.

DEPRESSION Awareness, Recognition, and Treatment (D/ART) Program
Department GL, Room 15c-05
5600 Fishers Lane
Rockville, MD 20857
1-800-421-4211
Web site: http://www.nimh.nih.gov/dart/darthome.htm#mission

Part of the National Institute of Mental Health (NIMH), the D/ART Program offers publications covering a variety of depressive disorders, including panic, anxiety, obsessive compulsive, post-traumatic, and phobic disorders. Specialized information available on depression includes depression in women, students, the elderly, and in the workplace. The recording accessed by the toll-free number is available in English and Spanish, and the NIMH web site is well done.

Eating Disorders Awareness and Prevention, Inc. (EDAP)
603 Stewart Street, Suite 803
Seattle, WA 98101
(206) 382-3587
Web site: http://members.aol.com/edapinc

A good starting point for information and educational resources on the prevention and treatment of eating disorders.

The Family Foundation Bipolar Network
1-800-518-7326

This organization offers a quarterly newsletter called the *Bipolar*

Network News. The toll-free number provides callers with subscription access, as well as gives information about other issues related to bipolar (manic) depression.

The Lithium Information Center
The Obsessive Compulsive Information Center
The Dean Foundation
2711 Allen Boulevard
Middleton, Wisconsin 53562
(608) 827-2390
Web site: http://www.deancare.com/info/info16.htm

These information centers feature an extensive library of references related to lithium (and other treatments for bipolar depression) and obsessive compulsive disorder. The staff will answer general questions by phone, and, for a small fee, will send information (articles, etc.) taken from their database of more than 35,000 references. This is a good source for lithium and OCD education.

National Alliance for the Mentally Ill (NAMI)
200 N. Glebe Road, Suite 1015
Arlington, VA 22203-3754
Helpline: 1-800-950-6264
Web site: http://www.nami.org/

The NAMI helpline provides callers with answers to general questions, access to literature on mental disorders (such as depression and schizophrenia), and information on how to reach state and local NAMI affiliates throughout the country. Members of NAMI benefit from a variety of services, including subscription to a newsletter, discounts on publications, and access to local support group events. The NAMI web site is well maintained and includes a NAMI membership application.

National Anxiety Foundation
3135 Custer Drive
Lexington, KY 40517-4001
(606) 272-7166

The National Anxiety Foundation provides a catalog of medical anxiety health information and nationwide specialists. Send a self-addressed, stamped envelope to the address above.

National Depressive and Manic-Depressive Association (NDMDA)
730 N. Franklin St., Suite 501
Chicago, IL 60610-3526
1-800-82-NDMDA (800-826-3632)
Web site: http://www.ndmda.org/

The NDMDA features a global network of 275 chapters and support groups related to depression and bipolar depression. Their mission is "To educate patients, families, professionals, and the public concerning the nature of depressive and manic-depressive illnesses as medical diseases; to foster self-help for patients and families; to eliminate discrimination and stigma; to improve access to care; and to advocate research toward the elimination of these illnesses."

National Foundation for Depressive Illness, Inc. (NFDI)
P.O. Box 2257
New York, NY 10116
1-800-248-4344

The NFDI can provide a free referral list of physicians and support groups in any geographic area, as well as a bibliography that lists available books, videos, and newspaper articles relating to depression. To receive either of these or additional information, send a self-addressed, stamped business-size envelope to the address above. Donations to the Foundation are welcome, but are not necessary to receive information.

National Institute of Mental Health
Office of Public Inquires
5600 Fishers Lane, Room7c-02
Rockville, MD 20857
(301) 443-4513
Web site: http://www.nimh.nih.gov/home.htm

A good source for information on a variety of illnesses, including eating disorders, panic, anxiety, and obsessive compulsive disorders.

National Mental Health Association (NMHA)
National Mental Health Information Center
1021 Prince Street
Alexandria, VA 23314-2971
1-800-969-6642

The toll-free line provides access to free information on more than 200 mental health topics, and a directory of mental health associates in any area is also available. Calls are answered by a recording, although there is an opportunity to speak with a live representative.

Obsessive-Compulsive (OC) Foundation, Inc.
P.O. Box 70
Milford, CT 06460-0700
(203) 878-5669
(203) 874-3843 (recorded information line)
Web site: http://pages.prodigy.com/alwillen/ocf.html

The OC Foundation is a friendly nonprofit information and referral agency specializing in obsessive-compulsive disorder. The Foundation offers three newsletters, the *OCD Newsletter, Kidscope* (for children), and *Check It Out* (written for support group leaders). Persons interested in being added to the mailing list can call or write to the address above. The web site is helpful, and the text is offered in English or German.

Index

Italic page numbers refer to sidebar information and illustrations.

ML   12/0)